Thinking and Writing for Publication

A GUIDE FOR TEACHERS

BONITA L. WILCOX

Cambridge Springs,
Pennsylvania, USA

INTERNATIONAL
Reading
Association

800 Barksdale Road, PO Box 8139
Newark, Delaware 19714-8139, USA
www.reading.org

IRA BOARD OF DIRECTORS

Donna M. Ogle, National-Louis University, Evanston, Illinois, *President* • Jerry L. Johns, Northern Illinois University, DeKalb, Illinois, *President-Elect* • Lesley Mandel Morrow, Rutgers University, New Brunswick, New Jersey, *Vice President* • Gregg M. Kurek, Bridgman Public Schools, Bridgman, Michigan • Jeanne R. Paratore, Boston University, Boston, Massachusetts • Lori L. Rog, Regina Public Schools, Regina, Saskatchewan • Carol Minnick Santa, Montana Academy, Kalispell, Montana • Rebecca L. Olness, Kent Public Schools, Kent, Washington • Doris Walker-Dalhouse, Minnesota State University Moorhead, Moorhead, Minnesota • Patricia L. Anders, University of Arizona, Tucson, Arizona • Timothy V. Rasinski, Kent State University, Kent, Ohio • Ann-Sofie Selin, Cygnaeus School, Åbo, Finland • Alan E. Farstrup, Executive Director

The International Reading Association attempts, through its publications, to provide a forum for a wide spectrum of opinions on reading. This policy permits divergent viewpoints without implying the endorsement of the Association.

Director of Publications Joan M. Irwin
Editorial Director, Books and Special Projects Matthew W. Baker
Senior Editor, Books and Special Projects Tori Mello Bachman
Permissions Editor Janet S. Parrack
Production Editor Shannon Benner
Assistant Editor Corinne M. Mooney
Editorial Assistant Tyanna L. Collins
Publications Manager Beth Doughty
Production Department Manager Iona Sauscermen
Supervisor, Electronic Publishing Anette Schütz
Senior Electronic Publishing Specialist Cheryl J. Strum
Electronic Publishing Specialist R. Lynn Harrison
Proofreader Charlene M. Nichols

Project Editors Matthew W. Baker and Shannon Benner

Cover Design Linda Steere

Copyright 2002 by the International Reading Association, Inc.
All rights reserved. No part of this publication may be reproduced or transmitted in any form or by any means, electronic or mechanical, including photocopy, or any information storage and retrieval system, without permission from the publisher.

Library of Congress Cataloging-in-Publication Data
Wilcox, Bonita L.
   Thinking and writing for publication : a guide for teachers / Bonita L. Wilcox.
     p. cm.
Includes bibliographical references and index.
   ISBN 0-87207-499-4
1. Authorship. 2. Academic writing. 3. Educational publishing.   I. Title.
   PN147 .W49 2002
   808'02—dc21

2002001758

To my mother, Edna Mae Johnson Southworth

CONTENTS

PREFACE vii

CHAPTER 1
Becoming a Writer 1

CHAPTER 2
Connecting Thinking and Writing 21

CHAPTER 3
Organizing and Sharing Our Writing 49

CHAPTER 4
Writing a Book Review as a First Publication 65

APPENDIX
Sample Charts, Guidelines, and Letters 79

REFERENCES 87

INDEX 93

PREFACE

> The danger is accomplishment. Once we learn how to do something, the tendency is to keep doing it. We lose the terror of early days and become content. We no longer fail and therefore escape the essential instruction of failure. We take no risks. (Murray, 2000, p. 191)

How many times have you said to yourself, "I could have written that book or article"? Have you thought about why you didn't? Often we are apprehensive about writing for publication because of faulty thinking. For example, we may think that we lack expertise, we may fear criticism from editors and readers, or we may feel certain that we have no time to write. Probably all writers have experienced these same fears, but fortunately many find the courage to overcome them. In fact, once we have been through the publication process, we are able to see that we do have expertise, criticism can be helpful, and we do have the time to write.

For many years, I struggled with the writing for publication required for promotion and tenure at the university level. I felt totally unprepared. I did not know how to begin, I had no research agenda, and I had not been engaged in purposeful knowledge-base building. My expertise was all over the place. As I began reflecting on my own learning, focusing on my own interests, and gathering information on topics I had chosen, I gained a sense of direction. In short, I soon understood what it meant to construct one's own meaning and generate new knowledge. I learned that there were personal and professional benefits in writing for publication beyond promotion and tenure, beyond fame and fortune. Writing for publication made me a better thinker, and better thinking made me a better teacher. I soon discovered that by sharing my own writing experiences, I could help others to become better thinkers and better teachers just by writing for publication.

In *Making the Journey: Being and Becoming a Teacher of English Language Arts* (2000), Leila Christenbury writes, "You are from day one a teacher making a journey. But the paradox is that from day one you will continue to become, evolve, and change as a teacher" (p. 4). It is the same for the writer. From day one you are in the process of both *being* a writer and *becoming* a writer. However, in my early attempts at writing for publication, I gave little attention to learning *how* to write. I thought it was a given: If one is a writer, one must know how to write. But this is not true. Writers must always be learning how to write. While in his seventies, Donald Murray, winner of a Pulitzer Prize in journalism, wrote, "I am forever grateful that I will never learn to write but that I will keep on learning" (2000, p. 191). Further, Murray claims, "We think by writing" (1996, p. 15), and he explains in more detail,

> Writing, in fact, is the most disciplined form of thinking. It allows us to be precise, to stand back and examine what we have thought, to see what our words really mean, to see if they stand up to our own critical eye, make sense, will be understood by someone else. (1984, p. 4)

Thinking for publication, just as writing for publication, implies that we begin with the end in mind so that we move through a process of reflection and revision with direction. Writers reflect (think about their thinking) to find their own meaning and to refine their understandings; writers revise (think about their writing) to make their meaning clearer to readers. Just thinking does have merit, but thinking about our thinking deepens our understandings and increases our mindfulness. Sharing our writing with others—and articulating and defending it—improves our thinking skills as we become more mindful of how teaching and learning happen. When teachers read, write, think, and share, they gain expertise and develop as professionals.

You may be thinking, "That's fine, but how do I get through that first publication?" This is a good question. It reminds me of a rainy day when I was painting my living-room walls. My kindergartner son asked, "Can I help?" After the "no" and "why not," I responded, "You really don't have enough experience with painting."

"Well," said my son, "how will I get the experience if you don't let me try it?" Wouldn't it be wonderful if we all had that kindergarten attitude toward learning?

If you have no idea about what to do first, *Thinking and Writing for Publication: A Guide for Teachers* will tell you where to begin. If you have tried writing and feel that you failed, this book will give you some direction toward getting back on track. If you feel you have nothing to write about, this book will show that thinking to be faulty. If you feel that you have no time to write, this book will offer some management and organizational suggestions to save time and energy with writing projects. Best of all, this book is a professional development tool intended to help you keep track of your learning as you sharpen your skills and build a knowledge base in order to become a better teacher and thinker through writing.

More specifically, here is an overview of what you can learn from reading this book. Chapter 1 highlights the personal and professional benefits of writing for publication. It suggests that a starting point for becoming a writer is to make writing a habit, to set goals, and to find a writing buddy. As you begin to gather evidence of your own expertise, you will see that professional development is a natural occurrence when the goal is to publish one's writing.

Chapter 2 shows you where to get ideas and how to make your thinking visible. This chapter focuses on evidence of your thinking, self-assessment of your thinking, and strategies for improving your thinking. It may even convince you that thinking about thinking and connecting ideas is almost automatic. You will see that paying more attention to thinking is the first step toward continuous improvement in writing. Furthermore, you will see that nurturing your habits of mind (dispositions toward thinking and learning) and monitoring your ways of knowing (approaches to thinking and learning) will facilitate the prerequisite thinking you must do before submitting a piece of writing for publication.

Chapter 3 suggests a way to organize a writing life. Developing a writing project and finding support for successful and unsuccessful efforts is also covered in this chapter. Whether book writing or journal writing is your interest, writing from the heart, instructional writing, and research writing offer numerous publishing possibilities for teachers. You will see that keeping current in your field is not so difficult, but nevertheless, it is essential for successful journeying in teaching or writing. Whether you intend to just write your personal history or to make your private writing public, you will learn the value is in the process.

Chapter 4 discusses one form of professional writing—a book review—and offers things you need to consider before you submit a review for publication. It suggests the best way to get started, and how to find an audience. It offers several examples of book reviews, and shows you how to self-assess your writing with a rubric. Finally, it answers questions relating to the preparation and submission of a book review.

In the Appendix, you will find sample charts for analyzing and keeping track of thinking skills, guidelines for writing a book review, and sample letters for submitting a book review.

Practice assignments are interspersed throughout the chapters; these are intended to activate and improve dispositions and approaches to thinking and writing. Completing the assignments will help you gain experience toward becoming a published writer.

When it comes to writing for publication, many believe that perseverance and commitment are more important than knowledge and skill. This book will guide you through the cognitive processes, but success will depend on your personal and professional commitment. You may have to change some of your behaviors, and there will be many hurdles. When it comes to thinking and writing, most of us don't get them right the first time. Good thinking, like good writing, requires fine-tuning and a continual honing of skills. However, if you are persistent, you, too, can join in professional conversations through writing for publication. So, are you ready to try it?

Acknowledgments

I would like to thank all the students and teachers who have shared in my teaching and learning experiences through my 50 years in classrooms. Also, I sincerely appreciate the support of my family, especially my husband, Jim, who actually *gave* me the time to write this book.

I would also like to thank the publications staff at the International Reading Association, and especially Matt Baker who offered encouragement, advice, and choices at just the right time to ensure that the final draft was much better than the first. Finally, I would like to acknowledge Barbara S. Vought and Debora Misencik for their book review contributions.

CHAPTER 1

Becoming a Writer

> The first lesson in making writing easy is to write every day. Habit is far more important than talent. If it is your habit to write—usually at the same time and place—then you will write. (Murray, 2000, p. 198)

In *Writing for Professional Publication: Keys to Academic and Business Success* (1999), Ken Henson claims his book "is written for people who are committed to self-improvement and who want to enhance their professional and personal lives" (p. 6). He reviews the many reasons to write for publication. You can write what you choose to write. You can write when you want to write. You can gain expertise and earn recognition. You can write creatively or share your research with colleagues. You can write to get tenure, or you can write for money. Writing to clarify thinking, to interact with and advance your profession, and to reach personal goals are the right reasons for writing for publication. Marsha Grace (1999) writes, "Writing is power. It can generate new energy and it can be a catalyst for personal change and enlightenment. Writing is reaching out, taking risks, exploring the world, and shaping the future" (p. 60).

This chapter begins with a story about my development as a writer, making it easy to see the difficulties teachers may have in becoming writers. Rarely is the school culture conducive to teacher learning, as teachers are isolated in classrooms with little free time. This is very different from the college campus where faculty members are *expected* to read, write, think, and discuss with colleagues. Still, teachers must be responsible for their own professional development. One sure way to make a focused effort toward continuous improvement is writing for publication. Developing a writing habit, setting goals, gaining expertise, and having a commitment to write are primary objectives of teachers who want to write for publication. This chapter focuses on getting you started and keeping you going in writing.

My Journey to Published Writing

As a novice classroom teacher, I rarely had time to think about joining in professional conversations. In fact, I had been teaching for many years before I understood this concept. My teaching career began in a rural Pennsylvania high school in the late 1960s, before portfolios, mentors, and the Internet. With 30 credits in my discipline and limited teaching experience, it was a struggle to survive.

Through trial and error I gained some expertise, and after several long years I adjusted to being a teacher. But personally, from my current perspective as a seasoned teacher with tenure, this was a time of great discontent. With a master's degree and several years of successful teaching, I felt stuck at the top with no place to go. It never occurred to me that other teachers felt that way too. Thirty years later, I read a research study that found "little opportunity for advancement" to be one of the reasons 30–50% of teachers quit within 5 years (Gregorian, 2001). Looking back, I think I could have written my way out of my discontent, but I was not, as yet, a writer.

During the 1970s and into the 1980s, there was a great deal of talk about the lack of learning in schools, but reformers focused on student learning, not on teacher learning. Teachers at that time seemed satisfied that 4 years of college and many years of classroom experience were adequate preparation for a lifelong career in teaching and learning. It was hard to understand how schools could be expected to mass-produce student thinkers and learners, when schools provided few opportunities and little encouragement for teachers to be thinkers and learners. Teachers had little input and no choice about professional development needs. Leaders in education began urging teachers to be in charge of their own professional development, but they didn't tell them how.

One day early in June of 1986, at the start of summer vacation, I received a scholarship to attend the National Writing Project's 5-week writing institute at a local college. The Writing Project leaders required participants to read books on teaching writing, keep a writing journal, share their writing, and apply what they were learning to their present teaching situation. I read books by Peter Elbow, Toby Fulwiler, Erika Lindemann, Donald Murray, Gabriele Rico, and Linda Rief. I recorded the authors' words, my reflections, and lessons I learned and discussions in which I participated during the institute. At the start of the institute, I was pretty sure that I was the only writer in the world with an empty mind, but from these written conversations I was able to fill my mind with ideas. I wanted to hear voices and have ideas like all the other writers I had read about that summer. When the institute ended, I continued to read books about teaching, write in my journal, share my writing, and try new strategies. The writing institute had changed my teaching/learning life. Although I was 100 miles from a university, when school opened in the fall, I was already enrolled in a doctoral program.

Unlike the situation in K–12 public schools, professional development at the university level is essential for promotion and tenure. Faculty members are in charge of their own professional development. Assistant professors are under tremendous pressure to publish. "Writing aids instruction" (Cramer, 2001, p. 268), just as research and methods do. Tenure and promotion committees seem to believe that you may be an effective teacher even if you are not a published writer, but if you are a published writer, it is much more likely. Sharing scholarship with students is important, but sharing scholarship with colleagues is especially valued. Junior professors understand that "published works are the currency with which we purchase tenure, promotion, salary increases, and the respect of colleagues" (Olson, 1992, p. 50).

I will be the first to admit that moving from private to public writing was a challenge, especially with all the other responsibilities of college faculty. I remember the frustration of not having time, the fear of my writing not being good enough, and my envy of those who had mentors and writing buddies. I also remembered some good advice: "Write the kind of thing you read" (Holmes, 1993, p. 15). My journal was full of ideas from books about teaching writing, private writing, and writing for publication. So that is where I began, and my first article, "Getting Published: Private to Public Writing" (Wilcox, 1996), was published in a major journal in my field. Believe it or not, the first one is the most difficult.

After several publications, I honestly believed that I was addicted to writing. I think this because when I didn't write, I was irritable and uneasy. I looked forward to the writing and to the excitement of seeing the published piece. Each piece seemed to come out of the one before it, and often I was writing several pieces at the same time. My list of publications grew longer as I gained expertise, and I gained expertise as my list of publications grew. I started to teach a course in writing for publication, and many of my students became published writers. Now, I am writing this book about writing for publication. You may be thinking that I was just lucky or that I have a lot of talent, but the truth is that I was determined, and I just sat down in my chair and wrote and wrote and wrote. Through perseverance I became a published writer, and you can be a published writer, too.

> **ASSIGNMENT 1**
> Find a pleasant place to write. Keep basic writing tools in your chosen place. Write at the same time each day. Begin with 15 minutes a day or with 30 minutes 3 times a week. Consider this writing to be "private" writing. You do not have to share it with anyone. Write as quickly as you can without being concerned about errors. It is important to tell the truth, however, so be as honest as you can be. Write about a "good day" in your life, a frustrating situation, or a childhood memory.

Why Don't More Teachers Write for Publication?

Teachers say their number one reason for not writing for publication is that they don't have time. Unfortunately, no one has time to write, but published writers take the time. They cultivate a writing habit and set writing goals. Ronald Cramer (2001) notes, "The journey into writing begins the day you make a commitment to write. Writers learn to write by writing. Like any skill, time must be invested in what you are learning" (p. 266). I recently read *Get Organized, Get Published: 225 Ways to Make Time for Success* (Aslett & Cartaino, 2001) to see if I could find some new strategies for moving minutes in my busy schedule. Through some organizational tips, I was able to save time usually spent searching for items. When it comes to writing, "Changing your habits is the most effective—and least expensive—way to save time" (Reno, 2000, p. 22).

Another popular excuse for not writing is, "I am not very good at writing." I have used this excuse many times, too. When I first started keeping a journal, I wrote in pencil so I could erase my mistakes before someone saw what I had written. I was hesitant to show anyone a piece of my writing because I feared criticism and rejection. Donald Murray (1996) writes, "But all of us question our talent, our creativity, our ability to write well enough to earn a reader's attention" (p. 11). Perhaps the traditional English-teacher attitude of correcting errors was stuck in my head instead of the idea of scaffolding to help a writer move writing to a higher level.

Still, every writer needs a reader. Take advantage of readers closest to you even if they aren't writers. My husband easily finds troublesome constructions that I would never imagine were confusing. He never marks misspelled words with a red pen, but a question here and there tells me I need to make the writing clearer. A colleague may respond, "So what? Doesn't everybody know this?" These kinds of responses are necessary and valuable because they send us back to the writing feeling confident that we can rethink and further develop our ideas.

Even the most critical reader can offer excellent advice. Academic journal editors are knowledgeable about current topics in the field; they are published writers and they know their audience. I have learned to respect rather than fear these editors. The ones I know work hard, know the field, are skillful communicators, and offer helpful suggestions for improving submissions. Book editors, however, have other issues to consider; for example, they must consider the costs of publishing a manuscript when they make acceptance decisions. Book editors often work collaboratively with other experts, and they "take advice, study the competition, read journals, absorb topical material from the mass media, attend conferences, surf the Net…" (Germano, 2001, p. 73). Editors are always attentive to the needs of their authors. Few manuscripts are published as submitted. Editors know the right questions to ask the author to make meaning more precise. They know just what to suggest to make a piece more acceptable to readers, and they know how to prompt authors to think better and write better so that a publication-ready manuscript results.

A third reason I often hear for not writing is, "No one I know writes for publication." Obviously, you can't get advice about writing for publication from teachers who are not published writers, but even novice writers can be good writing partners.

Writing with a partner may offer the additional courage to begin, and it is a great way to get published. With a writing partner, we seem to be more willing to take risks. Years ago I had trouble getting my proposals for conference presentations accepted. I found a "buddy" interested in the same kinds of topics, and together we were more successful than either of us had been alone. If you have ideas and you are a good thinker, finding a writing buddy could be just what you need. Sometimes, two heads are better than one.

Teachers who don't write are experts at listing their reasons for not writing. In *Crafting a Life in Essay, Story, Poem*, Donald Murray (1996) writes about writers who don't write, writers who don't finish their writing, and writers who don't submit for publication. Murray makes the point that it isn't that they can't write—it's that they don't. This is a common problem with teachers. Many want to be writers, but they just don't write. Many get started, lose interest, run out of time, forget where they left off, and just don't finish. Others actually finish a piece, but they fear rejection and don't submit. Sometimes, they submit and get rejected, and don't resubmit. If you want to be a published writer, you must write, you must finish, and you must submit.

There is, indeed, one very good reason why many teachers do not write for publication—they just don't know where to begin. This was true in my case. I knew why I wanted to join in professional conversations, but I just didn't know how. I did know the necessity of reading books, and I was able to find two books: *Resources for Writing for Publication in Education* (Katz, Kapes, & Zirkel, 1980) and *Publishing in English Education* (Judy, 1982). Both books were informative, but they weren't enough to get me started. I was a secondary teacher at that time, not a college-level educator, and I needed advice just right for me. I knew there were courses on writing for publication offered at universities, but I lived too far away. There were seminars available at conferences, but few rural school districts would help pay teachers' expenses to attend a conference. Fortunately, the late 1980s brought some major changes in our educational attitudes as teacher knowledge and skill gained status. Teacher expertise became a valuable commodity.

During the 1990s, many books were published on writing for publication. Ken Henson wrote three books on the topic during this decade: *Writing for Successful Publication* (1991), *The Art of Writing for Publication* (1995), and *Writing for Professional Publication: Keys to Academic and Business Success* (1999). In 1991, James Baumann and Dale Johnson published *Writing for Publication in Reading and Language Arts*. These editors indicate that knowledge and understanding about writing for publication can be learned through experience. In 1992, Karin Dahl edited *Teacher as Writer: Entering the Professional Conversation*, and I thought this book had been published especially for me. Shortly after came *Teachers Are Researchers: Reflection and Action* (Patterson, Santa, Short, & Smith, 1993). In 1994, Jean Stangl's book *How to Get Your Teaching Ideas Published: A Writer's Guide to Educational Publishing* was directed toward classroom teachers. I believe that these kinds of publications help teachers find success in getting their writing published.

These writers and editors seemed to understand how important, yet difficult, it was for teachers to write and share their stories. They seemed to understand that the school environment was not conducive to teacher learning. They seemed to sense that teachers needed a scaffolding approach to help them become writers. Teachers who write helping teachers who don't has had impact. Writing for publication gives teachers insight into the student's writing process, it gives teachers credibility by demonstrating their literacy skills, it gives teachers a larger knowledge base from the additional reading and thinking, and it encourages other teachers (Crowe, 1992). Marsha Grace (1999) writes, "Becoming a person who writes is important; becoming a teacher who writes is essential" (p. 60).

Teachers can increase their chances of getting published if they have a mentor. During my years as a doctoral student, my advisor and mentor was Allen Berger, a well-published writer in the education field. Berger (1997) encouraged all educators to tell their stories by writing for publication. He claimed that information about educational issues in the news was often inaccurate. He considered teachers to be experts who should take the responsibility for keeping the public informed about educational issues. Through the years, Berger has continually encouraged my efforts, and he seems authentically pleased when I have even the slightest success in publishing my work.

In *The Art of Teaching Writing*, Lucy Calkins (1994) writes,

> Why is it that we give our students opportunities to read and write, time to pursue their own important projects, mentors who inspire and coach, chances to work in small response groups…and yet we do not give these same things to ourselves? When will we take our own learning seriously? (p. 517)

> **ASSIGNMENT 2**
> No more excuses! Let's get started. Who do you know who writes? Ask around your school. Look on the Internet. Join a teacher electronic mailing list. Search for a mentor or a writing buddy. Begin by making a list of everyone you can think of who might be a mentor or a writing buddy. Circle the names you think are most promising. Talk to these prospective mentors and writers. They may be looking for you, too.

Where Do I Begin?

Years ago I read *Positive Addiction* by William Glasser (1985), a book that made a tremendous impression on me as a parent and a teacher. The main idea in this book is that teaching or learning good habits is as easy as teaching or learning bad habits. As obvious as it seems to me now, at the time it was an "aha." I immediately tried to figure out how I could apply it to my own life. When we intentionally try to develop or improve our good habits, Stephen Covey (1989) suggests that we need three things: "Knowledge…the *what to do* and the *why*. Skill is the *how to do*. And desire is the motivation, the *want to do*. In order to make something a habit in our lives, we have to have all three" (p. 47).

Knowledge (What to Do and Why)

There are many ways to be knowledgeable. Most of us learn best with a hands-on approach. If you want to develop a writing habit, you have to begin to write. Write every day at the best time for you. My best time is in the morning. I allow 2 hours for daily writing, although during that time I may be reading, researching, thinking, or looking for a misplaced item. If you designate less time for writing, that is fine, but it may take longer to develop the writing habit. Begin by writing at least two pages every day. You can start by writing stories about yourself. I began by recording events in my life. Autobiographical writing is a good place to start, because we have gathered this information for many years. A chronological approach makes the writing flow quickly. Other options are reading a book and taking notes, researching a topic on the Internet and writing about what you learned, or thinking about new ways to solve problems and recording the strategies leading to solutions. You need not write for an audience; just write for yourself. Keep track of all your "private writing" and record the time and the date on each piece.

Skill (How to Do)

Find a place where you are comfortable, a pleasant place with good lighting. Some writers have favorite pens and blank books. Some writers like to use a computer to write in an electronic journal. I have lots of shelves near my computer for reference books. I arrange my work area so everything I may need is nearby. It is a good idea to ignore the phone during writing time. Tell your family and friends this is your private time.

Now for the most difficult part: Put yourself in the chair and start writing. Writing happens to be a skill requiring lots of practice. This is where writers begin—they sit down and they write. They write if they are tired. They write if they have something else that needs to be done. They write even if they have difficulty staying on task. As you develop a writing habit, your writing and thinking skills will improve, also. When you move toward publication, there will be new skills to hone through writing. But for now, focus on putting your thoughts on paper.

Desire (Want to Do)

This is probably the most important requirement for developing a writing habit. I wanted to be a writer for a long time; I thought about it, I wrote about it in my journal, I talked about it to my friends, and I had started to write several different pieces for publication. You, too, have the desire to write, otherwise why would you be reading this book? Unfortunately, "want to" alone can't bring success; you have to do it. Sometimes you can strengthen your "want to" by accumulating some knowledge about "why." You may want to ask yourself why it is you want to write for publication. This is a great prompt to begin developing your writing habit. The reason I wanted to write for publication is that I knew the value of teachers teaching teachers, not only because teachers really are the experts, but also because the reading, writing, research, and sharing make a teacher better—better at learning, better at teaching, better at thinking.

Now, it is time to gain firsthand knowledge and skill. Now is the time to experience being a writer. Remember, "When we say we're 'too busy' to do something, it usually only means there are other things we want to do more" (Aslett & Cartaino, 2001, p. 19). There is a secret that writers share: "Writing produces energy. It is the writing—the excitement of discovering what I didn't know I knew, the delight of craft, the satisfaction of sharing—that gives me the energy to write" (Murray, 1996, p. 26).

I used to waste my writing energy by putting off my writing; I would get a cup of coffee, call my mother, check my e-mail, play a few games of solitaire. Most of us have procrastinated like this. The best way to avoid this is to set goals. I set short-term goals and long-term goals. I learned about setting goals in the *The 7 Habits of Highly Effective People: Powerful Lessons in Personal Change* (1989), in which Stephen Covey writes,

To begin with the end in mind means to start with a clear understanding of your destination. It means to know where you're going so that you better understand where you are now so that the steps you take are always in the right direction. (p. 98)

ASSIGNMENT 3

Most of us have goals, things we would like to achieve in a certain amount of time. We have daily goals, weekly goals, and lifetime goals. If we record these goals, we can more easily see our progress and change our direction when we get off course. Set some specific short-term writing goals for yourself. Determine how you will know when you have made progress. This is called hard evidence, but it doesn't have to be in volumes. Be sure your goals are realistic. For example, if you have written two pages a day for two weeks, you might set a goal of writing three pages a day.

Gaining Expertise

Nearly everyone is an expert at something, but to write a piece for publication, you need some expertise on a particular topic that will interest a particular reading audience. Most teachers read journals to keep informed about their profession, and for this reason you should always read the publications for which you might want to submit an article. As you develop good writing habits and set writing goals, you will want to focus on the kinds of topics that match your interests with those of your reading audience. Once you decide on a topic, you are ready to gain expertise.

There are many ways to gain expertise. As a writer, you need to use them all. As a general rule, the more you know about a topic, the easier it is to write about that topic. For this reason, when students tell me they have writer's block, I tell them that they need to get more information on their topic. On the other hand, when I was writing my dissertation, I became inundated with resources and information. I reached a point at which I did not know how to proceed. This was not writer's block; this was total confusion! So, I have worked out a way to keep things under control. I "integrate my literacies" by keeping track of my reading, thinking, interacting, demonstrating, viewing, and writing. The idea of integrating literacies comes from whole language and constructivist approaches, in which students make their own meanings and deepen their understandings through literacies such as reading, thinking, interacting, demonstrating, viewing, and writing. Strengthening reading strengthens thinking, strengthening thinking strengthens interactions, and so on (Wilcox & Wojnar, 2000).

Reading
Reading is necessary to gain new knowledge and new perspectives. Whether the texts are compendiums of basic skills and teaching strategies, individual texts on innovative approaches, or handouts from professional journals, new information and new ideas lead to new understandings that continually change. Learning usually begins with reading.

Thinking
Reflective thinking allows us to make our own meaning and generate our own understandings as our knowledge base changes and grows. Keeping track of thinking is usually done in a journal. The journal is a place to trace your thinking, take risks, explore, build, and re-create perceptions.

Interacting

Defending what we do, justifying the way we think, and articulating our ideas and understandings enable us to see more clearly what we know and how we came to know it. Thoughtfully prepared records of conversations with others can extend our knowledge base, improve our thinking strategies, and lead to deeper understandings.

Demonstrating

Applying new information, practicing new skills, and reflecting on the effectiveness of our delivery leads to continuous improvement. Systematic self-assessments illustrate significant differences between traditional lessons and "best practice" lessons. Experimenting with new strategies is often referred to as action research, and it offers teachers opportunities to generate new knowledge.

Viewing

Graphically representing what we think and know clarifies our thinking and enables us to interpret new information more easily and accurately. Visual texts using electronic media offer additional opportunities for teachers to learn and to share. A visual representation allows us to see relationships and make connections that otherwise may go unnoticed.

Writing

Private writing actively promotes thinking, but writing for publication usually represents the capstone experience in which all literacies come together. Prior knowledge has been assessed, new knowledge has been integrated, and current knowledge can be demonstrated. Thinking has been defended, extended, presented, and refined. George Hillocks Jr. (1995) writes,

> When we speak, we posit ourselves as persons with beliefs, memories, motives, and aspirations, none of which exist independently of the others. The person is the integration of all these and more, and our writing derives from the product of that integration. Since those beliefs, memories, aspirations, and motives change from moment to moment, we find ourselves in a constant state of reintegration, or reinventing ourselves, as it were. (p. 22)

In a nutshell, this is how it works for me. *As a reader*, I gather information on my topic. I take notes from books, write summaries, draw ideas, and design my own graphic organizers. *As a thinker*, my ideas continually change and are re-created. Looking from different perspectives, my ideas get tossed around. Through reflection I gain insight and can make better judgments about what and how I think. *As I interact with others*, I state my position and prepare for a defense. I listen to the arguments of others. Sharing ideas and peer assessments move my thinking forward. *As a demonstrator*, I can experiment and study audience response. I can readjust and test again. *As a viewer*, I know the importance of visual literacy skills, and I use maps, charts, diagrams, and illustrations to see more clearly and to show others what I mean. *As a writer*, I extend my thinking and gain deeper understanding through private writing. I share what I have learned and what I understand through formal writing. I submit a piece for publication after many drafts and look forward to even more transitions in my thinking that may require a higher learning curve. But none of this happens exactly as I have outlined; it is much more spontaneous. Thinking goes on all the time, more or less, and so do reading and writing. Interaction and viewing can occur anytime. Demonstrating is usually done in sequence, with thinking and viewing as necessary components.

    No one can deny that gaining expertise and building a knowledge base for continuous improvement is what professional development is really about. Monitoring and managing one's own professional development involves setting and accomplishing goals, as well as organizing and keeping track. But professional development depends on more than a commitment to learning; we need to be able to show evidence of quality thinking and learning. A piece of published writing can be strong evidence of professional development.

Before beginning Assignment 4, think about how you, as a teacher, gain expertise about teaching and learning. Think about the books you have read, the arguments you have made about issues, decisions you have made collaboratively, your classroom experiences, projects you completed, and other accomplishments. You are in charge of your own professional development. Isn't it time to gather some evidence?

> **ASSIGNMENT 4**
> Think about something you are an expert at doing—perhaps playing golf, quilting, woodworking, or antiquing. Think about how you got to be an expert. What did you read? What did you think? Did you talk to others? Did you show someone how? Did you make a drawing or illustration? Did you write anything? Write the answers to all or some of these questions. Then, think again about your expertise as a teacher and a learner, and describe in writing how gaining expertise depends on "integrating our literacies"—reading, thinking, interacting, demonstrating, viewing, and writing.

Am I Ready for the Challenge?

Somerset Maugham has been quoted as saying that "good habits are much easier to give up than the bad ones" (Reno, 2000, p. 21). Changing habits takes time and practice, but it is probably your mindset that matters most. Writers develop good writing habits through practice, and a little effort can sometimes go a long way. But monitoring and managing our own professional development takes a tremendous effort. Teachers are busy people. You will need to make a commitment. If you truly believe that writing for publication is key to your personal and professional development, then continuing to gain expertise will not be difficult for you.

Most of us spend a considerable amount of time building a knowledge base. We begin before we start school, usually we take an information leap in college, and then our learning curve levels off as we settle into a job. But learning is a lifelong endeavor, and being tenured does not ensure that a teacher is a lifelong learner. As we gain experience through practice, we become more knowledgeable, but that does not ensure that one is a professional, either. To be professional, we need to be a part of professional conversations—this requires background knowledge, experience in the field, awareness of current issues, and lots of thinking. Professional conversations can take place at conferences, through electronic mail, in Internet chat rooms, or when reading and responding to books and journals. When teachers are professionals, they join the "generating" information mode, and they create new knowledge through research, writing, thinking, and presentations. Gathering information, honing your skills, and sharing with colleagues are prerequisites to generating new knowledge. When your written work has been published, it becomes part of the professional literature.

You will gain expertise quickly if you focus on reading and recording what you find most interesting. Because you are already reading this book, it is a good place to start. Record your book notes, your dialogue with others, and your own thinking in a blank book, commonly called a journal. When you quote directly from the text, indicate the source and page. (Always do this when taking notes because writers must document the ideas of others.) Responding and questioning in your own words will deepen your understanding and extend your thinking. Occasionally, you will want to come to some conclusions as a way of closing before moving on to another topic. Articulating your thinking and defending your ideas will give you confidence. Later, you may decide to present a workshop or write an article, but for now you need to do plenty of writing to gain expertise.

If you were to look in my journal, you would see the following goals I recorded some time ago:

1. Make a commitment to read and write every day.
2. Take your project with you wherever you go.
3. Keep on trying, even when you feel like giving up.
4. Keep track of your progress.
5. Record your own history.
6. Read books and articles on writing for publication.

The amazing thing is not that this list is in my journal, but that I do these things almost automatically. These have become habits. I read and write every day. I rarely go anywhere without my book or journal. I have filled many journals recording what I have read, thought, and written. As Marjorie Holmes (1993) observes, "To qualify for kindergarten in the long, hard school of writing," you must "establish regular working habits" (p. 13).

As you strengthen your writing habits, it is important that you keep your writing organized and in one place. This is most easily accomplished using a journal. Perhaps you already have a journal. Perhaps you have been writing in journal a long time. Perhaps you have never written in a journal. In all honesty, I do not know of a single writer who does not keep a journal or a notebook. One thing is certain, none of these journals look alike. Journals come in all sizes and colors. They come with lines, or little squares, or with plain white pages. There is no age limit on journal writing, either. In *The Writer's Journal: 40 Contemporary Authors and Their Journals*, Sheila Bender (1997) tells the reader, "There is no wrong way to keep a journal" (p. 345). Also, as I have written in another publication, "The journal is a place where our thinking can become visible, a place where we toss around ideas, consider what others think, make connections between new and prior knowledge, examine our own thinking strategies, and judge our own learning" (Wilcox, 1998, p. 350). So, if you haven't already done it, the time has come to write in a journal.

> **ASSIGNMENT 5**
> Buy a journal to store all your thinking and writing. Your journal will show evidence of your reading, writing, and thinking. A journal enables you to view your learning patterns and to see how you make meaningful connections. You will be better prepared to articulate and defend what you think. Share your ideas and thoughts with colleagues, but you need not share your "private" writing, yet.

What Did I Learn?

I hope that you learned many of the benefits of writing for publication, and many of the reasons that teachers do not write for publication. It seems clear that writers write, and you must cultivate a writing habit. A mentor or a writing buddy could certainly support your writing habits. Setting and monitoring goals keeps you on task and moving in the right direction. Then, there is the matter of commitment—commitment to learning and to sharing. And, finally comes the question, Wouldn't you like to join in professional conversations? If the answer is yes, a journal is required as we move toward becoming better writers and thinkers.

CHAPTER 2

Connecting Thinking and Writing

> The most important writing is done away from the writing desk, when your unconscious and subconscious are playing with the subject. When you have an assignment to deliver on deadline, take some time to sit back and think about the subject. (Murray, 2000, p. 18)

Teachers, like good writers, know about the close connection between thinking and writing. Did you ever get a beautifully written answer to an essay question, but the answer was totally incorrect? Or, have your students lost points because poor writing made their thinking incomprehensible? Students sometimes seem totally unaware of any connection at all between thinking and writing. It may surprise you to know that published writers sometimes purposefully separate thinking from writing. Donald Murray (2000), for example, refers to thinking before writing as *rehearsing*:

> If I had three hours to deadline, I'd rehearse for an hour and a half, write for an hour, edit for half an hour; if I had an hour, I'd rehearse for thirty minutes, write for twenty, edit for ten. (p. 18)

Annie Dillard (1989) refers to this thinking before writing as a *vision*, comparing the writer and the work to the painter and the canvas: "You know that if you proceed you will change things and learn things, that the form will grow under your hands and develop new and richer lights" (p. 56). She explains that this process comes before you "begin to scratch out the first faint marks on the canvas, on the page" (p. 57). Even Ernest Hemingway has been quoted as saying, "My writing habits are simple: long periods of thinking, short periods of writing" (quoted in Murray, 1985, p. 220).

I can assure you that before published writers get to the point of separating thinking and writing, they have done a lot of messy connecting of thinking and writing. Publication does not happen without lots of messy thinking and writing. This chapter explores the concept of the "thinking journal" not only as a place to hold our thinking and writing, but also as a place where thinking becomes visible. By looking for evidence of different kinds of thinking, levels of thinking, and the language of thinking, teachers can quickly self-assess the quantity of their thinking. The chapter ends with suggestions for discovering, improving, and assessing our ways of knowing and habits of mind.

Making Thinking Visible Through Reflective Writing

Even though most of us think that we are pretty good at thinking, we would not miss an opportunity to improve our thinking strategies. We are reasonably sure that we cannot take it for granted that thinking skills automatically improve with practice. It does seem possible that our thinking would never improve much if we continually practiced poor thinking strategies. Classroom teachers, especially, must sharpen their thinking skills and improve their thinking strategies to be better thinking models for students, because students will more likely observe and imitate a teacher's straight-thinking strategy than follow a command to "think straight."

The process of "thinking about thinking"—also called metacognition or reflective thinking—helps us to better grasp our understandings through internal and external dialogue. Louann Reid and Jeffrey Golub (1999) write, "Reflection involves stepping back and objectively considering one's performance, whether it's classroom teaching practices, or one's own writing efforts" (p. 181). There is plenty of evidence indicating the positive effects of reflective thinking for teachers (McLaughlin et al., 1998; Rogers & Danielson, 1996; Seifert, 1999). In fact, David Perkins (1995), a Harvard researcher, has suggested that we can increase our IQ by practicing reflective thinking strategies. That might give us incentive!

One highly recommended strategy for reflective thinking is reflective journal writing, discussed in the next section of this chapter. By writing our thoughts and ideas in a journal, we make our thinking visible. We can change our journal entries, revise them, add to them, develop them, or criticize them. When we record our thinking regularly in a journal, we begin to see patterns and growth over time.

Let's take a look at how reflection might look as an actual journal entry. This example is from my private writing journal. It is an example of the kind of free-writing exercise I do occasionally with my students. I seem to be having a conversation with myself—not out of the ordinary for me when I do this kind of writing. I know I will revisit this journal entry at a later time, and I will be able to "see" what I thought as a starting point in the process of extending my thinking and gaining expertise.

I am really in a bad mood to do this writing today, but I know I must write. Instead of writing what is really on my mind, I am going to force myself to write what isn't on my mind. Maybe Peter Elbow had a good idea about how to use writing not as a mental catharsis, but as a way to redirect one's thinking. Let me see. I would like to write something about mentoring, but I can't imagine starting one more project. Still, we need to extend in order to accomplish. Students really have trouble grasping that concept. I suppose it would certainly require a lot of reading. Try justifying a lot of reading to students, "We need to read a lot first, because the more we know about our topic, the easier it is to write about our topic." Of course, they claim that they do not have time to read. Interesting. One reason many writers never get published is that they don't stop reading to get the writing done. This is quite a different problem than that of students who write without reading. How can they even consider writing informatively without reading? I contend that their lack of reading results in poor thinking. Imagine how students would react if I proposed, "All right class, we shall sit and think for the next 30 minutes." Students, and colleagues as well, would argue that sitting and thinking is a waste of class time. We really do take thinking time for granted. We believe the class should be learning something, but we don't recognize that practicing better thinking is *something*! When I was a kid living in the country, if you were found reading—you were thought to be on the lazy side. Lazy, in a working middle class family, was considered a bad practice. So at a young age I reasoned that reading out of school was not a noble activity. I suspected that sitting and thinking was even worse. My teachers labeled it "daydreaming." I wonder how we get to be better thinkers, if we aren't cognizant of the fact that we were practicing "fuzzy" thinking from the start?

    You may wonder what I learned from writing this piece. Let's look at my reflective thinking after I wrote the entry. For me, journal writing—just like thinking—is developmental, and an entry can work as a building block, moving me toward more thinking and inquiry. At the same time, a journal entry gives me an opportunity to take stock of where my thinking was at that time. In the beginning, I mention a "bad mood" and I remember that I was angry with my students for not understanding the difference in first drafting and final drafting. This was a graduate writing class with engaged students. It never entered my mind that they would submit quickly written pieces off the top of their heads without thinking about content or refinement. I had told them, "The first draft, you write it down. Second draft (the big one), you add content. The third draft, you 'fix it up.'" My assumption was that they would make excuses about lack of time for reading. I immediately connected their lack of reading to their lack of thinking. Here is where the writing was evidence of my own faulty thinking. Still, as the entry continued, I was able to make a more reasonable connection between reading and thinking from my personal experience.

When I reread the piece, I knew that I needed to do something to help my students. I developed a few writing exercises to show students how much easier it is to write when you have lots of information. I would "show" rather than "tell" them that writers must read. The second thing I knew immediately was that I wanted to think, write, and learn more about "fuzzy" thinking. Reflecting on what I had written resulted in a totally new learning experience for me.

You may be convinced that we can learn from our own writing, but do you believe that writing can make you a better thinker? I could tell you how this happens, but I think it would be better to show you. Mark Levy (2000) writes, "When you 'go with a thought' you assume that a particular thought is true, and you take a graduated series of logical steps based on the thought" (p. 39). Consider the fact that even if you use the best logic, someone else might move in a different, still logical, direction. Whether novice or expert at journal writing, it is time for you to see if writing can really make you think smarter.

> **ASSIGNMENT 6**
>
> Write a two-page journal entry about a problem or situation in your classroom. Write quickly without looking back. Read what you have written and find a point where you could have reasonably taken a totally different turn. Write two pages from this point. One more time, write two pages about another possibility for solving the problem or improving the situation. Read through your six pages of writing and determine whether or not your thinking has been extended.

What Is a Thinking Journal?

Stephen Covey (1989) writes,

> Keeping a journal of our thoughts, experiences, insights, and learnings promotes mental clarity, exactness, and context. Writing good letters—communicating on the deeper level of thoughts, feelings, and ideas rather than on the shallow, superficial level of events—also affects our ability to think clearly, to reason accurately, and to be understood effectively. (p. 296)

When I was much younger, I wrote down things as an aid to memory. This worked great for tests and quick recall. Today, I write down things as an aid to understanding. When thinking is made visible through writing, we can think about our thinking, reflect on our reflections, and understand our understandings. Through the writing we can make our own meaning, either by incorporating and interpreting new information or by relating and connecting new information with what we already know. As our knowledge base grows and we change our thinking, a "thinking journal" allows us to revisit our writing, review what we recorded, and see where our reflections have taken us.

A thinking journal is a place to store interesting ideas, meaningful quotations, and good or bad thinking. The journal "incorporates book notes along with reactions to readings and writings, recorded thoughts from interactions, and personal reflections about new ideas and teaching strategies under investigation" (Wilcox & Tomei, 1999b, p. 12). The thinking journal also allows us to look at writing and thinking through a different lens.

Since the publication of *The Reflective Practitioner: How Professionals Think in Action* (Schon, 1983), an abundance of books and articles have been published on the benefit of thinking reflectively for teachers. In *Journey of Discovery: Building a Classroom Community Through Diagnostic-Reflective Portfolios*, Ann Courtney and Theresa Abodeeb (2001) write, "Continued questioning and reflection of the practices we implement will clarify, refine, and extend us through our own zones of proximal development" (p. 86). But experience is not sufficient to give a teacher the necessary knowledge and skill to respond to constantly changing school environments. In the words of John Dewey (1997), we see that reflective thinking "means judgment suspended during further inquiry" (p. 13).

For Stephen Covey (1989), we must "move on an upward spiral of growth and change.... Moving along the upward spiral requires us to *learn, commit,* and *do* on increasingly higher planes. We deceive ourselves if we think that any one of these is sufficient" (pp. 305–306). Generally, the upward spiral requires that teachers must be learners and thinkers as they continuously try to improve on what they do and how they do it. This can be done through recording our conversations and reflecting on them—conversations with authors, conversations with others, and conversations with ourselves:

- Conversations with authors—recording information and direct quotations from texts
- Conversations with others—sharing and defending your thinking
- Conversations with ourselves—reacting and responding with questions or comments

When these conversations are thoughtful, when the focus is intentional, and when we are engaged, the process of knowledge building becomes almost automatic. When you record these conversations in a journal, your thinking becomes visible.

Constructing and generating new knowledge is what scholars do. You may stop and ask, "Are we expected to be scholars, too?" The answer is if you have to think and do as a scholar, you are a scholar. Your process might begin with new input (notes from a book), then you might respond to these new ideas (questions and comments), and finally you may articulate and defend these new ideas as you interact with others. Reflecting on what we know and what we still need to learn (monitoring and managing learning) is important. Often, we need to explore and expand our thinking before we find practical applications for what we have learned (personal connections). Constructing our own meaning requires that we connect what we already know with new information, and that we intentionally activate it (articulate and apply). As we continue to generate new knowledge, keeping track of these dimensions of thinking can lead to better thinking and deeper understanding.

Constructing meaning (building a knowledge base) from professional conversations is exciting. In Chapter 1, I introduced the concept of "integrating our literacies" through reading, thinking, interacting, demonstrating, viewing, and writing. It is the way we learn. Let's say you heard Donald Graves, a well-known authority on reading and writing instruction, speak about "letting youngsters write" without worrying about correcting all their errors. This sparked your interest, so you read two of Graves's books about teaching reading and writing to children (reading). Then, you recorded these ideas and reflected on them in your journal (thinking). You began to share these ideas with colleagues, asking for their comments, questions, and opinions (interacting). Again, you reflected and recorded while your brain made automatic connections (thinking). Later, you wrote an article about how you could incorporate ideas from Graves into your classroom (writing). When the article was rejected, you tested your teaching ideas to find supporting evidence (demonstrating). Finally, you prepared a poster to share with other teachers at a conference (viewing). By this time you will have expanded your professional knowledge base and gained significant expertise. When learning is recorded in a thinking journal, it is easy to see change and growth in thinking.

    Whether we call learning scholarship, renewal, or moving to a higher plane, using a thinking journal to keep track of our conversations, articulate our understandings, and demonstrate our thinking in these ways results in chronologically documented learning. In other words, we write our own history of learning, filling in pages one at a time. Being able to produce documentation of what one knows and can do is beneficial, and when we expand our collection to include all the artifacts we create, the collection becomes a portfolio. There are many publications on different kinds of portfolios, but the most helpful portfolios depend on the records and reflections easily kept in a thinking journal. To get you started in writing your history, you may want to review your response to Assignment 4 on integrating literacies before moving on to Assignment 7.

ASSIGNMENT 7

In order to investigate the way we learn, think of a topic you know a lot about. Draw a set of stairs diagonally on your journal page. On the "steps" enter the words *Reading, Thinking, Interacting, Demonstrating, Viewing,* and *Writing*. Try to determine how and when you learned to be so smart about this topic. Because your learning may not systematically proceed up or down the steps, you can add or change the guide words on the left. Remember this is still private writing, but you are trying to get a different view of how you gained some expertise. When you finish with the questions below, you might ask yourself, "What's next?" I'd like to see your answer!

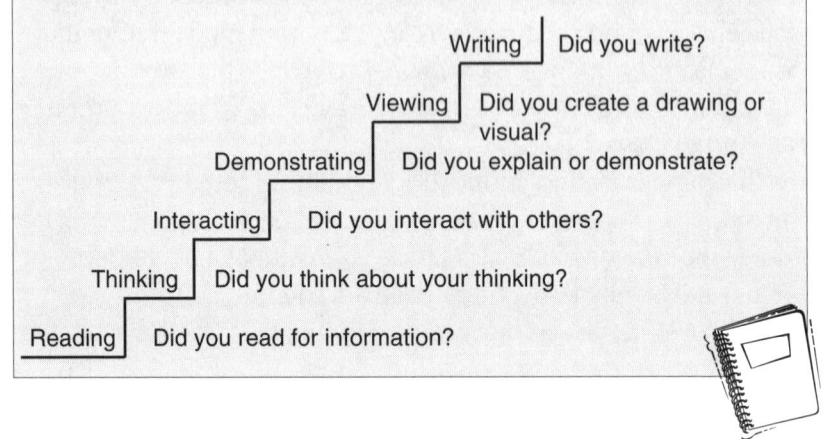

- Writing | Did you write?
- Viewing | Did you create a drawing or visual?
- Demonstrating | Did you explain or demonstrate?
- Interacting | Did you interact with others?
- Thinking | Did you think about your thinking?
- Reading | Did you read for information?

What Evidence Do I Look for to See How I Think?

As we begin to fill pages in our thinking journal, it is easy to see evidence of reading, writing, and viewing. Evidence of reading can be seen in our carefully recorded book notes. Evidence of writing can be seen in the number of pages we have written. Evidence of viewing may be seen in diagrams or illustrations showing our brainstormings or thoughtful interpretations. So far, we have been practicing writing. Now, it is time to look more closely at *thinking*.

First, we want to establish some guidelines to determine if thinking is in your writing. Later, we will establish some guidelines to determine whether the thinking is "good" or not. So, we will begin to look for evidence of quantity of thinking, not quality of thinking. This is an important distinction. To complicate the matter even more, we will look for three specific kinds of evidence—evidence of different kinds of thinking, evidence of thinking words, and evidence of higher order thinking. We will search, find, and record the evidence on charts provided in the Appendix.

Different Kinds of Thinking

To find evidence of different kinds of thinking in writing—basic thinking, critical thinking, creative thinking, reflective thinking, parallel thinking, and fuzzy thinking—start with the working definitions presented in Figure 1. If you don't agree with my definitions, the Internet is a good place to find some of your own. Paste these definitions in the front of your thinking journal. Obviously, the way we process information depends on the particular task or circumstances. Sometimes, we follow a specific procedure, such as the scientific method or a proof in plane geometry. Other times, thinking is exploratory or forced, as with some journal entries. Some thinkers work with accepted knowledge, using any of the many available building blocks (skills). Others prefer reorganizing knowledge, applying knowledge, or generating new knowledge. Most thinkers use the same skills for different kinds of thinking. For example, evaluating skills and focusing skills are useful for any kind of thinking.

In Figure 1, I present examples of skills required for different types of thinking. Keep in mind, however, that specifying thinking skills to a particular thinking process can

FIGURE 1
DIFFERENT KINDS OF THINKING

- **Basic thinking**: This kind of thinking has to do with finding a correct answer or making a decision based on accepted information. It requires information-gathering and focusing skills. Evidence can be found in writing that states the facts and moves toward a logical conclusion.

- **Critical thinking**: This kind of thinking has to do with organizing, connecting, and evaluating, leading to a specific conclusion. It requires organizing and analyzing skills. Evidence can be found in writing that presents accurate information and asks reasonable questions from prior knowledge and personal experience.

- **Creative thinking**: This kind of thinking has to do with synthesizing, extending, and imagining, leading to a new approach or idea. It requires elaborating and generating skills. Evidence can be found in writing that describes a new point of view or a different way of conceptualizing.

- **Reflective thinking**: This kind of thinking has to do with mental management and readjusting our habits of mind and ways of knowing, leading to intentional change and better thinking. This kind of thinking requires exploring and evaluating skills. Evidence can be found in writing that indicates control over the focus and depth of thinking.

- **Parallel thinking**: This kind of thinking has to do with collecting different views or approaches to a problem until "the full picture emerges" (De Bono, 1999, p. 12). It requires inferring and restructuring skills. Evidence can be found in writing that recognizes the strength of "mixed media" in solving problems, adding emotion, benefits, intuition, caution, and differing opinions.

- **Fuzzy thinking**: This kind of thinking is often unreasonable and illogical, not based on fact. It is common when we are too emotional, in a hurry, superficial, making excuses, or "jumping on the bandwagon." Evidence can be found in writing that is based on half the facts, either-or thinking, hasty generalizations, or oversimplification.

be limiting; good thinkers choose whatever skill is necessary to move their thinking forward.

Look back through your writing and search for occurrences of different kinds of thinking in the journal entries. Highlight the examples you identify with an orange marker, and record them on the chart in the Appendix (see page 80).

Thinking Vocabulary

Along with different kinds of thinking, we also need to consider the language of thinking. Shari Tishman and David Perkins (1997) write, "Just as the colors of an artist's palette influence the painting that emerges, the words we have available to us influence the way we think about the world, including the inner world of our own mental life" (p. 371). Most of us use and understand hundreds of thinking words, words indicating what we presently think, words indicating a specific thinking process, or words indicating a product of our thinking. For example, I *suspect* (epistemic stance) that we frequently encourage lower level thinking in school. *Investigating* (intellectual process) further, I surveyed a group of students. My *conclusion* (intellectual product) will be shared as a conference presentation.

I investigated my use of thinking vocabulary, and I made a list of all the thinking words I use in everyday conversations. Then, I searched my journal to find thinking words I used in my written conversations. Last of all, I made a list of thinking words from my reading, intending to incorporate them into my writing. I am constantly revising my list of words, and I am convinced that both my writing and thinking improve as I am able to be more precise. I am suggesting that we can be better thinkers and writers if we give more attention to and deliberately use words that describe our epistemic stance and intellectual process or product more and more accurately. I find thinking words through reading, put them in my written conversations, and almost automatically, they soon come up in everyday conversation.

Figure 2 contains a list of my thinking words, categorized as speaking, writing, and reading vocabulary. There are a variety of ways you can categorize thinking words. For example, I list words by present thinking, process thinking, and product thinking. Other times, I list thinking words as easy, more difficult, and most challenging. The point is that I am consciously thinking about thinking words, and I try to use them more accurately to effectively describe my cognitive

FIGURE 2
MY THINKING WORD LIST

From speaking	From writing	From reading
consider	ponder	cogitate
observe	outline	appraise
propose	speculate	assimilate
contend	perceive	postulate
grasp	emphasize	deduce
guess	discriminate	scrutinize
claim	investigate	extrapolate
wonder	infer	reminisce
estimate	contemplate	conjecture
reason	hypothesize	surmise
argue	research	corroborate
suppose	predict	envisage
inspect	theorize	ascertain
synthesize	deliberate	ruminate
describe	dwell	muse
suggest	integrate	glean
imagine	probe	evoke
defend	incubate	opine
justify	brainstorm	syllogize
decipher	differentiate	reticulate

activity. Barry Beyer (1997) writes, "One of the marks of good thinking and effective communicating is the use of clear, precise language. This is especially important in talking about the cognitive states and actions related to thinking" (p. 71). In the Appendix, you will find a chart on which to record your thinking words (see page 81), but first highlight them in your journal in green.

Higher Order Thinking

The last evidence we are going to consider is the level of cognition, more commonly known as the levels of Bloom's taxonomy. Benjamin Bloom (1956) outlines six levels of cognition: knowledge, comprehension, application, analysis, synthesis, and evaluation; the top four levels require higher order thinking skills. However, thinking can be of a high or low quality at any level of thinking. So, what I look for in my journal entry is the frequency of occurrences at a particular level, rather than "good" or "bad" quality of thinking.

Bloom's taxonomy has always been popular with teacher educators in teaching students to understand and write objectives. More recently, researchers look for ways to use the taxonomy for teaching higher order thinking (Slifkin, 2001; Wojnar, 2000). To find ideas on using Bloom to extend thinking, look on the Internet; you will find more information than you can imagine. Keep in mind that undocumented information on websites may not be accurate or reliable, but it can lead to valuable resources. Investigating levels of thinking also will be a hit with your students.

Figure 3 shows my interpretation of the taxonomy and how I use it for journal writing. I hope to find more evidence at the higher order thinking levels in my writing. At the same time, I can begin to look for quality in my own writing, at least at the extremes. For example, I can determine whether my

> **FIGURE 3**
> **LEVELS OF BLOOM'S TAXONOMY**
>
> **Knowledge: Recalling and remembering information**
> - Listing items
> - Using direct quotations
> - Writing definitions
>
> **Comprehension: Understanding information**
> - Explaining
> - Restating
> - Summarizing
>
> **Application: Adapting or using information**
> - Selecting and organizing details
> - Incorporating ideas or concepts
> - Relating concepts to new situations
>
> **Analysis: Dividing information into parts**
> - Looking at individual parts
> - Making connections
> - Finding patterns in similarities and differences
>
> **Synthesis: Integrating and creating new information**
> - Drawing an illustration of a complex idea
> - Reshaping information
> - Making a prediction
>
> **Evaluation: Judging the value of information**
> - Giving logical evidence to defend thinking
> - Offering accurate self-evaluation
> - Determining worth by balancing pros and cons

attempts at evaluation were thoughtful or mindless, or if my synthesis was closer to summarizing or conceptualizing. Often when I revisit my writing, I am able to see where my thinking went awry. Find evidence of the levels of thinking in your journal and highlight the examples with a yellow marker. Record your findings on the Higher Order Thinking chart in the Appendix (see page 82).

When I look at the evidence of different kinds of thinking, the language of thinking, and the levels of thinking from my journals over longer periods of time, I can see growth and change in the kind of thinking I do. Playing these kinds of "thinking games" motivates me to think more about how I think and how I might think better.

> **ASSIGNMENT 8**
> So, how many occurrences of thinking did you find? Summarize and record your findings in your journal. Using a table or a graph will make it easier to see patterns and make comparisons in the future. Hopefully, you will work toward increasing the occurrences of thinking in your journal. You may want to intentionally "stack the deck." This is fine because once you are aware of these thinking words, a snowball effect seems to take over.

How Can I Nurture My Habits of Mind?

Before becoming a published writer, I had to nurture my habits of mind. You may have trouble believing that I haven't always had a disposition toward thinking reflectively or a tendency toward being open-minded. Writers must cultivate their thinking habits to be more in line with the habits of the best thinkers. The first thing to do is to *reflect on your reflections*. David Hobson (2001) writes, "A journal is not just for writing, of course, it is also for reading. If kept over a long enough period of time, a journal can be viewed as a repository for a teacher's observations, stories, insights, and wonderings" (p. 24). Hobson goes on to explain that the strength of a journal is in the way "it leads itself along. It suggests, questions, identifies new areas to explore, reveals meaningful absences, and uncovers recurring patterns" (p. 25). First we record our perceptions and knowledge and then we reflect and assess what is in the writing. Sometimes we forget about reflecting and assessing what is in the writing, yet this is how the journal "leads itself along," and this is how journal entries link to become building blocks for the writer.

For example, if we go back to my "bad mood" journal entry (see page 24), I mentioned students' lack of reading. In a later journal entry, I wrote about how I begin to put an article together on a particular topic: I do lots of reading. Donald Murray (1984) suggests, "You can't write nothing" (p. 17). I wanted to show my students that this was true. This thread moves through many journal entries—why it was necessary, where the exercises came from, how I fine-tuned them, how well the exercises worked. This led to making the exercises better.

On the other hand, my entry started another thread of entries concerning fuzzy thinking. This led to my thinking and investigating what kinds of evidence could logically support my claim. This led to entries concerning evidence writers look for in their own writing to avoid fuzzy thinking. Traces of the fuzzy thinking thread appear in many entries. Where it will lead me, I don't know. Murray (1996) writes, "I have lived my life not once, but a hundred times in night dreams and day dreams, in imaginings and fantasy, in the essays, stories, poems I have told myself—and my readers" (p. 2). Whether in private writing or published writing, I believe that we first try to record or describe our perceptions. Then, we go back to reflect on the thinking in the writing. I *read to learn* from my private writing. I follow the threads. David Hobson (2001) writes, "One moves from a description of experience to a sort of commentary on it" (p. 22). In my thinking journal, I cannot distinguish between thinking and writing. It is such a mess—information and imaginings, experience and make-believe, facts and wishes. Yet, it is a comfort to know that what I know and how to find what I need to know is here someplace in my thinking journal.

The second thing to do to nurture your habits of mind is to *take risks*. Thinkers and writers are risk takers who need freedom to stretch and bounce. In *Bird by Bird: Some Instructions on Writing and Life*, Anne Lamott (1994) writes, "perfectionism will ruin your writing, blocking inventiveness and playfulness" (p. 28). I have to admit the critic in me used to try to fix the messy thinking and writing in my private journal. One reason I did this was because I worried that someone might read it—what would they think? Most of my concern, however, was focused on straightening my "crooked" thinking and filling in the gaps. I found that I rarely think in a straight line and my brain makes connections (actually it takes leaps) that even surprise me. This fixing-up process may have been good training for honing drafts intended for publication, but it slowed my thinking and writing. To nurture your habits of mind, let the writing flow freely. Free writing, private writing, and writing from a prompt are strategies that allow the mind to make automatic leaps. Try to ignore the critic in your head. Risk taking is essential to thinkers and writers.

The third thing to do to nurture your habits of mind is to *adjust your attitude*. It was nearly 100 years ago (1909) when John Dewey wrote *How We Think*. Dewey believed that students should be taught the scientific "attitude of mind and habit of thought." He went on to explain, "Knowledge of the methods alone will not suffice; there must be the desire, the will to employ them. This desire is an affair of personal disposition" (quoted in Wiggins & McTighe, 1998, p. 171).

Some time ago I owned and operated a quilt shop. I thought I knew everything I needed to know to successfully teach quilting. Jokingly, a friend asked me to take a quilting class with her at another quilt shop. "You might pick up some new strategies," she teased. Congenially, I did attend the class, improved my skills and knowledge, and reaped many other benefits. But the most valuable lesson I learned was about the improving. Through synthesis and analysis of our thinking habits, we can monitor the ways we approach new information and learning to determine when change might be appropriate.

In his book *The Thinker's Way: 8 Steps to a Richer Life*, John Chaffee (1998), a well-known expert on critical thinking, tells us that the best thinkers have lively, energetic minds and generally display the following qualities: open-minded, knowledgeable, mentally active, curious, independent thinkers, skilled discussants, insightful, self-aware, creative, and passionate. I am sure that most of us have some of these qualities. Other educators claim that

> high quality thinking is characterized by these attributes: Intentionality, Persistence, Deliberateness rather than impulsiveness, Precision, A desire to be well-informed, Seeking and giving reasons for evidence, Open-mindedness (suspending judgment), Objectivity, Willingness to change a position, and Judging in terms of situations, issues, purposes, and consequences rather than in terms of dogma, self-interest, or wishful thinking. (Beyer, 1997, p. 3)

I believe that a disposition toward thinking about thinking, a willingness to take risks, an open-minded attitude toward further inquiry, and a tendency to record and share evidence are essential behaviors of good thinkers. I think we can see these kinds of behaviors in ourselves and in others. Still, when it comes to the quality of thinking in a particular piece of writing, it is easier to look at more specific skills. For example, I created a rubric as a visual to allow me to see what I thought quality thinking might look like in my writing. My Rubric for Thinking in Writing (see Figure 4) offers a quick way to holistically self-assess my thinking. I have found that in a journal entry or in a quick-write, I might circle different bullets at different levels than I would circle in a finished piece

FIGURE 4
RUBRIC FOR THINKING IN WRITING

4 The best writer
- researches problems and finds alternative solutions
- formulates goals and creates products
- evaluates choices and assesses the consequences
- identifies main ideas and finds sequences
- prioritizes and recognizes fallacies
- compares/contrasts to identify relationships
- modifies and extends thinking
- summarizes and hypothesizes
- predicts and visualizes

3 A better writer
- senses a problem and decides on a variety of possible solutions
- assesses and revises products
- identifies issues and generates alternatives
- recognizes patterns and classifies information
- determines criteria and verifies information
- infers deductively and inductively
- shifts paradigms to extend and elaborate
- synthesizes and plans strategically
- speculates and imagines

2 A good writer
- recognizes problems and collects ideas from others to find a solution
- finds useful products as needed
- makes thoughtful decisions
- collects and organizes ideas when necessary
- gathers information before making a decision
- decides what might work and tests it
- searches for answers to purposeful questions
- uses problem solving strategies when necessary
- tries again if unsuccessful

1 A poor writer
- lacks problem-solving skills
- has no initiative to design
- refuses to make decisions
- claims that analysis takes too long
- thinks only smart people are logical
- sees evaluation as time consuming
- believes that synthesis is confusing
- understands that imagination is for youngsters who daydream
- fears that stretching one's mind is painful

prepared for publication. I know how to improve the quality of my thinking in my writing through thoughtful revision. But I wanted a self-assessing tool that would allow me to see improvement and to offer evidence of quality in writing that was not "fixed-up."

Before moving on to another kind of assessment tool, I understand that you may think differently than I do about the most important characteristics and skills of quality thinkers. Each of us must fine-tune our own notions of quality. However, it is easier to pinpoint quality when we look at the extremes. For example, it may not be as difficult to see the difference in the best writer and the poor writer in my rubric, as it is to see the difference in the good writer and the better writer. It is the same with thinking. We can see the differences more easily at the extremes.

Poor quality of thinking often depends on illogical conclusions and false arguments or fallacies of thinking. This brings us to the problem of transfer, which "occurs when a person applies knowledge or skills acquired from some earlier context in a new context" (Perkins, 1995, p. 223). Unfortunately, we sometimes transfer inappropriate knowledge and skill, causing a negative transfer. Negative transfer helps to explain why even smart people use hasty, narrow, or fuzzy thinking. This kind of thinking is commonly called *faulty thinking*. We need to be able to recognize the "fallacies of thinking" (Sebranek, Kemper, & Meyer, 2001, p. 445) in order to avoid them. Use caution here, because most of us let this thinking creep into our writing.

We still have not decided how to measure quality in our thinking or how to determine if it is even there. John Chaffee (1998) writes, "It is by questioning, making sense of, and analyzing that you examine your thinking and the thinking of others" (p. 35). Chaffee clearly states that we can judge the strength and accuracy of our thinking by evaluating the evidence that supports it. The strength and accuracy of the thinking depends on the strength and accuracy of the evidence. Chaffee (1998) suggests the following kinds of questions that critical thinkers often ask themselves when evaluating evidence:

- Authorities: Are they knowledgeable, reliable, and in agreement?
- Written references: What are the author's credentials? What is the evidence for the author's opinion?
- Factual evidence: What is the source? Is the conclusion supported?
- Personal experience: What are the circumstances? Were perceptions distorted? Are other explanations possible?

We certainly have a lot to think about. Evidence, it seems to me, is very important. How each of us defines quality thinking is also important, as is avoiding faulty thinking habits. Demonstrating skills in writing is important because "almost everyone agrees that writing ability relates directly to learning and to thinking" (White, 1985, p. xi). So, how does all this come together in a tool to indicate our quality of thinking? Actually, it is easier than you might think.

First, you list the characteristics of quality thinking that you have in your mind. Then, you decide what specifically makes that characteristic look like good thinking or poor thinking. Add the numbers 5, 4, 3, 2, and 1 underneath, and you have a scale to indicate quality. It may not be perfect, but it will work. You can change the characteristics. You can adjust the specific description. You can use it with all kinds of writing. I've borrowed this idea from Chaffee (1998), who uses this kind of a scale for self-assessment throughout his book. My scales for self-assessment are presented in Figure 5.

> FIGURE 5
> SCALES FOR SELF-ASSESSMENT
>
> **Thinking About Thinking**
>
> When I record my thoughts and reflect on my reflections, I move toward deeper understandings.
>
> I write down ideas so I remember what happened and what I was thinking about at that time.
>
> 5   4   3   2   1
>
> **Attitude Toward Learning**
>
> I wonder what I can apply to make my approach better.
>
> I know all this. I've heard it before. "Been there, done that!"
>
> 5   4   3   2   1

It is time for you to try the strategy. Think about people you know who are quality thinkers in your opinion. Ask yourself, "What makes their thinking so good?" And, you are on your way.

> **ASSIGNMENT 10**
> List three or four characteristics or behaviors of a quality thinker in your opinion. Let's say you choose "open-mindedness." You must think in terms of extremes. How does an open-minded person act? How do you determine when a person is not open-minded? Go ahead and make your scale. When you have finished, you will want to try it out and make adjustments. You might even risk showing your self-assessment scale to a friend.

What Did I Learn?

Understanding the thinking-writing connection is critical to becoming a published writer. This is because thinking and writing for publication requires a long-term commitment. We have started at the first level with messy thinking and writing in a journal. This you do for yourself. At the second level you are going to share with a reader, and thinking and writing becomes concentrated and focused. At the upper level of thinking and writing for publication is revision, where writers refine and clarify meaning with words. For now, we are still working at first-level thinking and writing, the most important level for both published and unpublished writers. Whether you are responding in a journal to a thinking/writing prompt, recording a discussion from lunch, or taking notes from a book you are reading, the more you write, the stronger habits you will cultivate. You have learned how to find direction and patterns of thinking in your writing. I'm sure you know that adding information and skills to your knowledge base is as essential to teaching and learning as it is to thinking and writing for publication.

Becoming a writer can also profoundly change your life as a reader (Lamott, 1994). Knowing how to judge the quantity of your thinking in writing and how to assess its quality should enable you to improve your ways of knowing and habits of mind. This is a giant step toward personal and professional development. Still, learning is a process, and for the most part, it isn't done in isolation. Reaching out to others through publication—the focus of Chapter 3—is also a necessary part of professional development.

CHAPTER 3

Organizing and Sharing Our Writing

> To be truly professional, teachers must develop their own beliefs and knowledge about what it means for teaching—and learning—to be "good." Given the nature of education, teachers' beliefs and knowledge will inevitably take account of ideas and recommendations from numerous individuals inside and outside the classroom. But in the end, all ideas must be constructed and "owned" by classroom teachers themselves. There is no other pathway to professionalism in education. (Seifert, 1999, p. ix)

As we observe our surroundings on our journey of becoming a published writer, we should be able to see plenty of evidence that we are writers and thinkers. We have established a time to write, and we are strengthening good writing habits. We have a journal that contains our private writing and thinking, and we have made a commitment to join in professional conversations. Now, we want to investigate ways to keep track of our projects and organize our writing life. We will want to learn about different kinds of writing opportunities and places to publish. Of course, if we can find support for our new ways of thinking and habits of mind, our progress will seem easier as we move toward writing for publication.

The Writing Portfolio

I have a simple way of keeping track of writing ideas, writing in progress, writing under consideration, and published writing. I do it with a writing portfolio I construct in about 10 minutes. I start with a pocket-file notebook and six folders. I cut enough off the edge of the notebook so that the folders fit more easily. I label each folder as follows: Reading Resources, Writing Ideas, Submitted Pieces, Current Project, My Published Pieces, and My Thinking Journal. Following are some examples of artifacts that might be found in each of these folders:

> Reading Resources: publication manual, articles about writing, lists of websites, books to read
>
> Writing Ideas: illustrations, journal analysis, quotations, ideas
>
> Submitted Pieces: book reviews, articles, proposals, queries
>
> Current Project: my project journal, related articles, drafts, correspondence, disk
>
> My Published Pieces: "How to eat an elephant a bite at a time" (*Animal Tidbits*)
>
> My Thinking Journal: prompts, clusters, entries, pictures, and drawings

In the Current Project folder, I keep all my thinking on and collection of materials related to this project—notes from reading and other conversations, target journal correspondence and guidelines, quotations and clippings, journal entries, related pieces I have written, and visual representations. On the Current Project disk, I keep an outline, a working draft, a list of references, and inserts.

In the front of my journals, I always list my goals. Setting goals allows me to focus on specific tasks and evaluate my progress. In the book *Write It Down, Make It Happen: Knowing What You Want—and Getting It*, Henrietta Klauser (2000) writes, "Once you start writing your goals down, the brain will send you all kinds of new material: innovative, energizing ideas for planning out and expanding those ambitions" (p. 53). I set my goals according to the time I have scheduled to work on the project. I know that gathering resources does not require the concentration and focus needed for second-level thinking and writing when I begin to write my first draft. Considering these kinds of details enables me to set more reasonable goals. Over time, I have improved my estimations and can more accurately determine how long my new adventure will take. My project journal allows me to compare time, strategies, and destinations from other projects. This gives me a better sense of direction, but I know that new projects bring new challenges and surprises.

If an occasion arises when you can benefit from sharing your writing portfolio, it is easy to transfer your artifacts to a poster for viewing (see Figure 6). Exhibiting your work in this way is an example of "representing to learn." It forces you to keep your portfolio up to date, and offers evidence of your development as a writer. I strongly recommend sharing your portfolio with others. The benefits are great and it is relatively easy to do.

A writing portfolio is much more than an organizing tool. It is a place to record your thinking and learning, your goals and achievements, your conversations and understandings. Keeping track of these kinds of cognitive activities "results in gaining new perspectives and stretching one's mind" (Wilcox & Tomei, 1999a, p. 7).

FIGURE 6
WRITING PORTFOLIO POSTER

Writing Portfolio

My Published Pieces

My thinking Journal

Reading Resources

Writing Ideas

Submitted Pieces

Current Project

Publication manual
- A book to read
- Related articles
- List of websites

Quotations
- Illustrations
- Journal analysis
- Clippings

Query letters
- Article
- Proposal
- Book review

Project Journal
- Drafts
- Notes
- Correspondence
- Disk
  - Outline
  - Working draft
  - References
  - Inserts

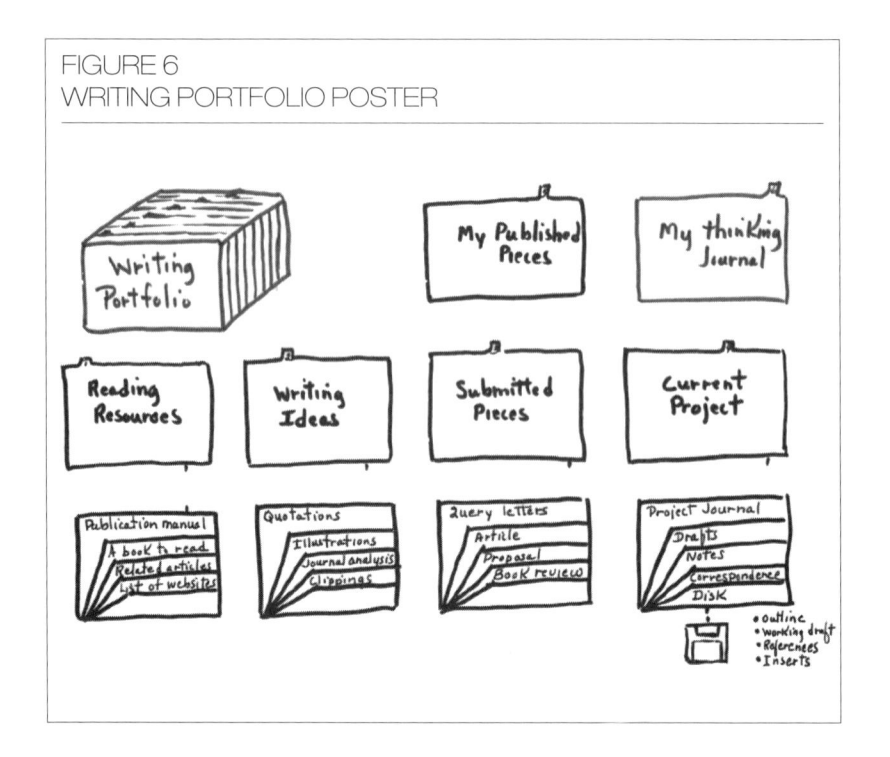

ASSIGNMENT 11

Build your own writing portfolio. You can do it easily with a pocket-file notebook and six empty folders. Use my labels or think of your own. Begin today to organize your writing and thinking artifacts.

Developing a Writing Project

Whenever I teach a course on writing for publication, I ask students to tell me how they organize individual writing projects. I can tell you from experience, everyone does it differently. I want to share my way, not because it is the best or because I think it will work for you, but because it works for me. I have been through periods of no method, tried a variety of strategies, and reached the conclusion that it is most effective to have some method. Here is how I prepare a piece for publication from start to finish.

Keep in mind that writers juggle their tasks and processes, and rarely is an approach truly linear. I weave in and out and move all around with automaticity. Sometimes I proceed quickly with little regard for clarity. Other times I write a word at a time, constantly changing what I thought I wanted to write. Sometimes the writing comes easy, but other times I cannot squeeze a coherent paragraph out of my head. I have learned my patterns and my limits. I drink coffee and play a couple of games of solitaire early in the day, in preparation for the two pages of text I will end up thinking is acceptable. Some days I write more, some days less, but usually I write only two pages (400 words). I spend about half my scheduled writing time with other documents—looking for quotes or facts, or something I want to mention or discuss. I do my share of research on the Internet, too.

Specifically, this is what you could do as you begin a new project. Start with an idea. Decide on a purpose (ask "So what?"). Gather background information (read, interview, survey). Talk to people (ask "Should I query?"). Draw some diagrams or charts (analyze and synthesize). Prepare a working outline (ask "Who cares?"). Find a target journal (check on guidelines). Write a first draft, and then write the "big" draft (increase the content). Then, write the "fix-it up" draft (fine-tune thinking and enhance the writing). Next, smooth it out (read it aloud). Ask someone else to read it. Revise again, to get the best draft possible (ask again "So what?"). Do your own assessment, and then submit (ask "Did you check the spelling?"). Does this sound easy enough?

Now, if you put all those tasks and questions in a hat, shake them up, and pull them out one at a time—that is the way I prepare a piece for publication. Georgia Heard (1995) writes, "Contrary to what I was taught in school, writing isn't a scientific formula: Think of a topic, make outline, write topic sentence, write introductory paragraph, then write the rest" (p. 56). You, of course, must discover your own way, but before you sit down to write your first piece, consider what the editor or publisher may be looking for in a submission.

First, the article has to fit the journal or the book has to fit the publisher. Look for a good match between the audience and the manuscript. Second, a publication must have appropriate content. A perfectly good piece of writing may not be good enough for a particular publication if readers are not given learning opportunities they expect. Third, you have to give accurate information and do citations correctly. When you quote another writer, do it correctly and always acknowledge the person's name. Fourth, the writing needs to be interesting and stimulating. Finally, if you wonder why I did not mention clarity or quality of writing, it is because there is an unwritten rule: *Thou shall not submit writing of poor quality.*

> **ASSIGNMENT 12**
>
> Just for practice, choose a topic for a book or a journal article. Find a publication that looks the way you think your finished product should look. Make a list of items to include in your hypothetical piece. Try to put your items in an appropriate order. Does this remind you of an outline? What kind of research do you need to do to fill in the blank space?

Finding Advice and Support for My Writing

My grandson Jascha was visiting while I was writing this book. As I worked at my computer, I noticed that he stopped to look at the bookshelves. "What do you think?" I asked. "Well," he began a little disgusted, "all your books are about the same thing." He is right, of course. I have many books on writing—teaching writing, evaluating writing, publishing writing, and research writing. But the books I love the most encouraged and supported me as a beginner. The books at the top of my literacy learning list were *Write to Learn* (Murray, 1984), *Writing Without Teachers* (Elbow, 1986), and *Teaching With Writing* (Fulwiler, 1987). Also, I have found the following Writer's Digest books to be valuable for novice writers:

> Cheney, T.A.R. (1987). *Writing Creative Nonfiction: How to Use Fiction Techniques to Make Your Nonfiction More Interesting, Dramatic, and Vivid*
>
> Clark, T., Woods, B., Blocksom, P., & Terez, A. (Eds.). (1997). *The Writer's Digest Guide to Good Writing*
>
> Edelstein, S. (1993). *30 Steps to Becoming a Writer and Getting Published: The Complete Starter Kit for Aspiring Writers*
>
> Emerson, C. (1993). *The 30-Minute Writer: How to Write and Sell Short Pieces*
>
> Holmes, M. (1993). *Writing Articles From the Heart: How to Write and Sell Your Life Experiences*
>
> Larsen, M. (1997). *How to Write a Book Proposal* (2nd ed.)
>
> Nuwer, H. (1995). *How to Write Like an Expert About Anything*
>
> Polking, K. (1987). *A Beginner's Guide to Getting Published*

The publishers of books and journals also offer support. In the case of journals in education, other teachers and teacher educators review articles for editors. When outside reviewers read for editors, the journal is said to be "refereed." In the case of books, usually experts in the field are chosen as reviewers. Editors give the reviewers' comments to the author with the hope that suggestions will improve the manuscript. It is a very informative learning experience to be a reviewer. It will even help inform your writing.

Workshops and writing classes can be very helpful to writers. It is almost like having a personal support group. Most universities offer writing classes for credit. The colleges hosting the National Writing Project advertise summer institutes for teachers (see http://writingproject.org).

If you cannot enroll in a course, you can always start a writing group of your own. Find several teachers interested in writing for publication and meet regularly. Begin reading and thinking and sharing. Joining an electronic mailing list where you can ask questions and make comments may boost your spirits, too. Support groups are important, but "Who will teach me to write?" asks Annie Dillard (1989) in *The Writing Life*. She continues, "The page, the page, that eternal blankness, the blankness of eternity which you cover slowly…that page will teach you to write" (pp. 58–59). Remember, when it comes to writing, you must eventually sit down by yourself and write words on a page.

If you are fortunate and have a writing buddy, get together regularly with a written agenda. If not, find opportunities to discuss teaching and learning with colleagues. In a study conducted by Linda Tafel and Joseph Fischer (2001), when teachers thought about "what influenced their learning about teaching and their professional development, many cited a colleague or mentor who both affirmed their learnings and nudged them toward other inquiry and self-discovery paths" (p. 231). You may not want to share your private writing with just any colleague, but focused conversations are advantageous. Don't forget to record and reflect.

In the long run, no matter how much support we get from our books and acquaintances, we may find our journey difficult at times. As a matter of fact, we may experience failure. As a child, I was taught that the greatest thing about failure was that it could help you to succeed. This is true in the case of rejection. Writers learn to live with rejection. If they are lucky, an editor will give suggestions to improve a particular piece. I always learn from a rejection letter, even if only that I should have sent my writing somewhere else. I prepare for a quick turnaround by targeting two journals, so if a piece is rejected by the first choice, I send it to the second choice. I try to have more than one submission under consideration, too. Then, if one is rejected, I still have hope for the others. When it comes to rejection, I keep a positive attitude. From my experience as a journal editor, I know it is usually not a personal decision, and it may not be related to the quality of the submission. I haven't done the research, but my guess is that more manuscripts are accepted the second time around.

Before we have to worry about rejection letters, we need some experience with constructive criticism. You have been expecting this, perhaps, and it is time to share your private writing with someone you trust and respect. Actually, he or she doesn't need to know a lot or have your kind of expertise. Ask the person to be honest with you, and choose the piece you share with care.

ASSIGNMENT 13
Ask your writing buddy to read a piece of your writing. If you can exchange pieces, that is even better. Keep in mind that praise may be less helpful than honesty. Reserve your judgment when you get a response. Don't say anything, just record the comments. It may take time to learn how you can benefit from sharing your writing. Begin now because we are moving quickly toward sharing our writing with complete strangers.

What Kinds of Writing Can I Publish?

Books and articles are published on all kinds of topics, so you should begin with topics you know best. Many classroom teachers find instructional writing a good place to start. A teacher might explain a great lesson idea in enough detail for a reader to present it to a different audience, or show the "how, what, when, where, and why" of the idea to allow the reader to have some success in presenting it. If you created special assignments or assessments for your lesson, you might share these in a way that the reader could copy and immediately use with other students. Resources can be listed as a sidebar so readers can easily find more information. I usually tell my readers why I was motivated to write in the first place.

Often teachers have pedagogical stories to tell, rather than a "how to" idea. If you have a favorite teaching or learning strategy that works well, write about your successes using it. Tell it like a story. Read a book and a few articles on the same topic to become familiar with the theory behind your strategy. This will add to your expertise and allow you to pass on more information to your reader. Nearly everyone loves a story, and a chronological approach organizes itself. I find that with stories, I have to cut many details because I tend to get wordy. When writing from the heart, words flow more easily for me. I take precautions so that the strategy is more important than the story. Keep in mind that it is common practice to be selective with the "telling," and on occasion you may choose to enhance your story for effect. You cannot stretch the truth when working with information and documentation, but when re-creating a story, you have some leeway.

If you are not comfortable with telling stories and sharing strategies, you could submit an informational piece of writing. Informational books are always popular in all subject areas. For example, you could take a variety of approaches—a guide telling how to do something, a biography of a famous person, a serious study, or an investigation. Take a trip around the bookstore—in person or on the computer—and visit the library to find more ideas than one can imagine. I have a friend who writes books while he teaches lessons. Each night a lesson becomes a chapter. At the end of a term, he has written a book. I have another friend who wanted to publish a picture book for adults. It is always helpful to find a publication that looks like or sounds like something you could write to use as a guide.

You will notice that some publications accept only research writing. If you are interested in writing research, find a good example to follow. Remember that targeting a research publisher is like targeting any other audience:

> Your readers will judge you by how accurately you judge them. If you misjudge how much background they need, if you offer your findings in a way that does not speak to their interests, you will lose credibility that every writer needs to hold up his side of the conversation. (Booth, Colomb, & Williams, 1995, p. 13)

Many teachers partner with university writers to coordinate and publish research projects. This is a good way to get started in research writing.

Another option is to read a current publication about teachers as researchers, such as *Teachers Doing Research: The Power of Action Through Inquiry* (Burnaford, Fischer, & Hobson, 2001). This book will answer your questions about different kinds of inquiry. Team up with another teacher with similar interests, and learn and write together. Remember that experienced researchers use a different format than practitioners sharing a research experience. You and a colleague could develop a writing relationship for life.

You also might consider writing and publishing outside of academe. Submitting to a more general audience is always an option. You may want to inform the general public about educational topics, or you may have an idea for a bestseller. Recently I published a personal article in a magazine unrelated to education. The topic was close to me, and I wrote from experience. Still, I did research and took many photographs. Then I prepared a chronological view of the topic. This may not be considered a "professional conversation," but it gave me additional practice and insight into writing creative nonfiction for publication.

> **ASSIGNMENT 14**
>
> Because writing a book is frequently more complicated than writing an article, it is smart to check out all that is required before investing the time. Read a book about "how to write a book" or get to know an author. As a trial run, practice with a short children's book. Do the illustrations yourself. Keep it informative. Be creative. When it is completed, test it on a real reader. Later, you may want to revise and submit it for publication.

How Do I Find Outlets to Publish Different Kinds of Writing?

The most likely places to publish or to join in professional conversations are by writing articles for the journals in your field. Most writers write for the journals they read. Depending on your reason for writing, it is important to know whether the intended journal is refereed. If an article appears in a refereed journal, it usually indicates that reviewers read and responded to it. When an article appears in a nonrefereed journal, it is an editor's decision. Most journals publish a list of intended themes or monthly topics as well as guidelines for authors. As is the case with well-known journals, all the information an author needs is available on the publisher's website.

Your teaching association might publish a list of affiliate journals. These are regional and state journals in your field. Many feel that their chances for publication are better in less competitive journals. The smart writer is more concerned with audience and purpose than with competition. Also, writers must consider whether to publish online or in hard copy. An online journal has a quick turnaround of 2 to 4 months, whereas the normal time for moving through the publication process with hard copy can be significantly longer, 9 to 12 months. Some journals publish only online. Others put their published journals online after distribution to subscribers. Some journals are only available in hard copy. If your submission is timely or more appropriate for an online medium, you might want to consider an online journal.

Another place to look for places to publish is the Educational Resources Information Center (ERIC), available to students, teachers, and researchers around the world. Through ERIC, you can access 16 databases. Here you can find information, look at journal publications, or submit your own writing. ERIC has a variety of clearinghouses, including reading, English, and communication skills; teaching and teacher education; assessment and evaluation; social studies and science; elementary and early childhood education; and information and technology. In many countries, journals are expensive and articles are difficult to acquire. ERIC is available online, and instructors and researchers can order copies of articles online at a reasonable price.

It is amazing how many journals are available to educators. Let's say I wanted to write a piece on portfolio assessment for secondary teachers. Perhaps I got an idea from an article I had read in *The Reading Teacher* (an International Reading

Association [IRA] journal for educators teaching children ages 5–12), but my expertise was in secondary language arts. I might investigate the kinds of articles in IRA's journal for secondary teachers, *Journal of Adolescent & Adult Literacy*, or I might look for a related piece in the *English Journal*, a publication of the National Council of Teachers of English (NCTE). If I wanted to reach a larger audience of K–12 teachers in all disciplines, I might consider *Educational Leadership*, a publication of the Association for Supervision and Curriculum Development (ASCD). If I were competent with computers and multimedia, I would look for articles on my topic in *Reading Online* (http://www.readingonline.org), an electronic journal from IRA. Because of the many possibilities for publishing in education, it is recommended that you prepare manuscripts for the journals you read, especially in the beginning.

At the same time, it is important to have more than one place to publish in mind, because when rejection comes, the best policy is to revise and resubmit. Most teaching organizations publish more than one journal. IRA publishes several print journals, one journal that is exclusively online, and a newspaper. NCTE publishes many journals covering all levels of teaching and learning in English language arts. I submitted my first "real" journal publication to the *Journal of Adolescent & Adult Literacy*, but it was actually published in *The Reading Teacher*. I would not have sent the piece to the other journal if the editor had not suggested that I do. Still, after many publications, I have difficulty saying that I do have one piece that no one wants to publish. I just keep sending it out.

There is no shortage, either, of places to publish books. Many universities have their own presses, and teacher organizations publish books on teaching and learning. Many large publishing houses specialize in books about teaching and learning. Others publish textbooks. Educators have many choices. I suggest finding a book like the one you want to write and do some research on the publisher. Book publishers are very different from journal publishers, and a wise writer will investigate the publishing house before submitting a manuscript.

For guidelines on book publishing for teachers, go to the websites of international and national education organizations. Most websites offer a complete description of what you must do to submit a book proposal. You will even find forms and advice. Book publishers are always well represented at conferences, too. Usually, you need only to ask the person working in the booth for author guidelines. You can learn a lot from writing a book, but keep in mind that it is a time-consuming project; it requires lots of information and writing and thinking. Although it is a comprehensive project, many teachers begin their writing career with a book proposal.

There are several publications written specifically for educators looking for places to publish. *Cabell's Directory of Publishing Opportunities in Education* (Cabell & English, 1998) is one. *The Writer's Handbook* (Burack, 2001) offers advice for writers and lists conferences on writing, state arts councils, and organizations for writers. Check the reference section of your library for others.

ASSIGNMENT 15
If you do not already subscribe to a teacher's journal and receive a current catalog of publications through your professional association, do this now. Although you can share with other teachers or go to the library, it is better if you own these resources so you can use them as artifacts. You can cut them up or store parts in subject folders for future thinking and writing endeavors.

What Did I Learn?

Documenting our professional development can be time consuming, but by tracking and recording our learning, we write our own history. In *Organizing From the Inside Out: The Foolproof System for Organizing Your Home, Your Office, and Your Life*, Julie Morgenstern (1998) introduces the Kindergarten Model of Organization: Divide the space by activities, focus on one activity at a time, store things where they are used, label clearly, and keep a visual of the arrangement. Using this model for systematically checking our progress is quick and easy with a writing portfolio.

We also learned about projects and focusing on particular topics. We discussed where to look for support and where to look for opportunities to share writing. We have made progress in filling in pages of the history of our learning. We have begun to share our private writing with a person we trust. Still, we may worry about a greater threat—sharing our thinking and writing with strangers. Here the chance of rejection often seems greater than it is. To limit our risk of rejection, we are going to begin with a book review, which I discuss in the next chapter.

CHAPTER 4

Writing a Book Review as a First Publication

> Book reviews provide a valuable service to a field of study, they offer a means of making useful contributions to a field, and they are an efficient scholarly writing activity if one is already doing the careful reading essential to good reviewing. (Erwin, 1992, p. 111)

This chapter looks closely at a specific type of publication—a book review—and the similarities and differences in the writing process and the publication process this form of writing might require. A book review is a logical first publication because most of us read books, a book gives us something to write about, and we have all had practice in school with book reports. Of course, book reports were written for our teachers, and most of us gave little attention to audience. Book reviews, however, require careful consideration of audience. Preparing a book review for submission takes a writer through the steps of the publication process, making it easy to see how it relates to the writing process. After reading this chapter, your final assignment will be to submit a book review for publication. Although the task may seem overwhelming, you will be able to do it by taking one step at a time.

Why Begin With a Book Review?

There are several reasons for beginning with a book review. All the basic "truths" of writing seem to be evident in this one short, uncomplicated writing project. Beginning with the writing process itself, there are three things to consider: (1) We all have our own writing process; (2) the writing process is messy and not really linear; and (3) our personal process varies with the writing task. Still, most writers generally follow an order much like this one from *Write for College: A Student Handbook* (Sebranek, Meyer, & Kemper, 1997):

- Collect and focus your thoughts (prewriting)
- Generate an initial version of your writing (drafting)
- Improve upon your writing (revising)
- Prepare it for submission (editing/proofreading) (p. 3)

    The writing process is always a part of the publication process. However, the publication process involves specific procedures determined by the writing task. The six-step approach to writing a book review, which is discussed in the text and assignments throughout this chapter and presented in its entirety in the Appendix (page 83), outlines specific procedures to follow for this particular task. This six-step approach has worked for me, it has worked for many of my students, and I think it will work for you. However, every book reviewer has a personal publication process. Publication processes differ as much as writing processes. You may change your ways of doing things as you gain experience.

    Another reason to begin with a book review is that it is always a good idea to start with what you know. Most of us were asked to write book reports in school. However, book reports are often summaries, lacking higher order thinking about content. This is a major difference between book reports and book reviews. A book review is not a summary, but a synthesis, dependent on higher order thinking about content.

Perhaps the best reason for beginning with a book review is that the writer already has a topic and information as soon as the book has been read. Writing nonfiction requires information gathering, because "writer's block is invariably the result of too little research" (Poynter, 2000, p. 94). Difficulty in finding a topic and gathering information is directly related to the complexity of the writing task, so the book review is a relatively easy piece of writing. Book reviewers need not be overly concerned about gathering information and writer's block. If you read a book carefully and follow the six-step approach, you will have plenty of information to write a thoughtful book review.

Finally, the idea that we learn through writing can only be understood when we have experienced it firsthand. We must allow our personal experience to help us. A book reviewer always chooses a book carefully. I try to review books on topics I like and know something about. This facilitates making my own meaning from personal connections I make with the new information in the text. Many writers claim that they don't know where the writing is going until they see what they say. For me, writing is always a surprise journey; I have to wait until I get to the end of my trip before I can see how I got there. Learning through writing also depends on how we gather information (book content) and how successful we are at integrating it.

ASSIGNMENT 16
Step 1: Annotation—Read a book of your choice. Highlight or underline as you read the text. Make comments or ask questions in the book margins.

"Eating an Elephant": Publishing Your Book Review One Step at a Time

Writing your first publication may seem a lot like "eating an elephant." Have you read the poem "Melinda Mae" by Shel Silverstein? The poem is about a little girl who said she would eat a whale. She took little bites and she chewed very slow, and in the end, Melinda met with success and ate the whale. You eat an elephant the same way—a bite at a time. Let's take a look at how a bite at a time translates into one step at a time.

If you look closely at the chart in Figure 7, you will see that writing a book review for publication requires lots of prewriting. You may have thought that prewriting was not that important. Actually, it is the thinking up front that determines how easily the reviewer moves through the steps that follow. The prewriting steps enable a book reviewer to collect and focus his or her thoughts (annotation, note taking, illustrating, and making meaning). Then, the drafting/revising step to

FIGURE 7
BOOK REVIEW VERSUS GENERIC WRITING

Writing process for a book review	**Generic writing process**
Annotation	Prewriting
Note taking	Prewriting
Illustrating	Prewriting
Making meaning	Prewriting
Composing	Drafting/revising
Revision/submission	Editing/proofreading

generate an initial version and revise it (composing) will be much easier. Last, the process ends with the editing/proofreading step (revision/submission). In the chart, it is easy to see the relationship between a generic writing process and a writing process for the publication of a book review.

You may wonder why so much emphasis is on prewriting. It is because thinking and prior knowledge are essential ingredients of good book reviews. Although most reviewers begin with an objective summary, a deeper understanding is necessary.

Connie Emerson (1993) writes, "The more subjective reviews require additional thinking time, since the emphasis is on the reviewer's reaction to and evaluation of the book" (p. 159). After making meaning by extending their interpretations of the book, book reviewers are ready to compose.

ASSIGNMENT 17

Step 2: Note taking—After reading your book, go back through the text and record important and/or interesting quotations and ideas in your journal. Stay close to the text. Indicate exact page numbers in your journal. Add your own reflections as your mind makes automatic connections for you.

Step 3: Illustrating—Draw a graphic or visual representation of the whole book. Take a look from the balcony to see the "big picture." (Close your eyes and pretend you are looking at the situation from a higher place.) A different perspective can give you insight.

Step 4: Making meaning—Think about the practical applications and usefulness of the content in the text as you extend your interpretation. Try reading some of your favorite parts aloud. Spend some time thinking and allow your brain to "bubble." This may help you find direction for your writing.

Composing: Choosing an Audience and Drafting the Piece

Choosing an Audience

Seasoned book reviewers know that audiences appreciate an honest and accurate review. Readers are especially appreciative if the review saves time (they don't have to read the book) or if it saves money (they don't have to buy the book).

I write book reviews for other teachers. This limits my audience some, but not enough. For example, this book was written for teachers, but more specifically, it was written for teachers who want to write for publication. If I wanted to review a book for the same reading audience, I might choose to review a book about writing for publication. On the other hand, if I choose to review a book about strategies in teaching the English language arts, I would have to identify a different teacher audience—an English-teacher audience, perhaps.

Where do we look to find our target audience? Finding an audience was difficult for me when I decided that I wanted to write a piece for publication. All my previous writing was private; I had no audience. But getting published meant "'going public'—going from virtually no audience to a totally unknown, unimaginable audience" (Wilcox, 1996, p. 361). The concept of audience presented a roadblock, and it took all my courage to get over it. At first, I was "unwilling to put myself and my writing at risk…standing alone with an unpublished piece had overwhelmed me" (p. 364). With time, I learned that I needed an "in between" audience. This audience was a small group of colleagues who offered friendly feedback.

Today I am much more confident when it comes to identifying an audience. So after I have chosen a book to review, I usually begin looking at a journal that publishes reviews on books like the one I have decided to review. Then I read several issues of this journal and a variety of reviews to get a sense of what is acceptable for publication. If I think the journal is a match, I adopt the same audience as this journal. Usually, I write for journals I read regularly. This saves time, because writers need to know their journals. Submitting to an unfamiliar journal usually results in a letter of rejection. Never submit to a journal you have not read.

Keep in mind that in some respects you still do not know your audience. Even after you have targeted a journal and read several issues, your audience is still unknown. Who are these readers? What will they think? Will they write a letter to the editor about your review? Is this cause for alarm? Writers know that different readers respond differently. All readers will not read your review. Of those who read it, all of them will not agree with it. They may not even like it. Nevertheless, it is a comfort to know that you are in the right ballpark, and that it may not be possible for the book reviewer to really know the audience.

Drafting the Piece

The sample book review that follows illustrates the way I might begin to draft a review:

> McLaughlin, M., & Vogt, M.E. (1996). *Portfolios in teacher education*. Newark, DE: International Reading Association.
>
> I recently reviewed several books on portfolios in teacher education for a column in *The Reading Teacher* (Wilcox, 1997): *Teacher Portfolios: Literacy Artifacts and Themes* (1996) by Rogers and Danielson with a focus on the evidence of personal learning; *How to Develop a Professional Portfolio: A Manual for Teachers* (1997) by Campbell, Cignetti, Melenyzer, Nettles, and Wyman with a focus on meeting competencies in regard to standards; and *The Teacher's Portfolio: Fostering and*

Documenting Professional Development (1996) by Glatthorn with a focus on supervision and assessment. This book, *Portfolios in Teacher Education*, focuses on the connection between instruction and assessment.

With this kind of an introduction, the reader knows that the reviewer has some background knowledge on the subject of teacher portfolios. For teachers interested in this particular kind of a portfolio, I have suggested three other sources with different perspectives. In addition, if readers were to look at the reviews I wrote on these related books, they would be able to make a more informed decision about which book they want to read or want to buy.

Continuing with my book review, I might write a second paragraph that looks like this:

McLaughlin and Vogt describe a portfolio process for both graduate and undergraduate students in a teacher education program. They explain the way two teachers successfully used portfolios with elementary and secondary teachers in reading methods classes. Their design, implementation, and assessment procedures are clearly illustrated, making replication of their course possible for interested teachers of reading methods.

After this paragraph, I would move into the structure of the text and mention chapter concepts. Usually, I try to find one idea that really made an impression on me, so I can show usefulness, applications, or both. Finally, I would go back to the first paragraph and connect it to my conclusion. The conclusion might begin, "These authors are already working with several others on a soon-to-be-published book, *Professional Portfolios for Teachers*...." I would attempt to limit my review to 400 to 600 words. I know I will cut around 100 words when I work on revisions. However, the number of words depends on the complexity and length of the book I am reviewing.

Finally, the review is ready to proofread, edit, and submit. It is necessary for writers to follow the guidelines for submission carefully. Journals print guidelines frequently or writers can download guidelines from a website. Not following guidelines is a bad practice, because your review may not be considered at all. Most reviews written for "teacher" kinds of publications are read only by the editor. Often, I ask another teacher to read my review. I find this very helpful.

Before submitting your review to an editor, you may want to send a query letter to ask if the editor would be interested in publishing your review. You can use this same kind of letter for an article. See the Appendix for sample query and cover letters (pages 84–85).

ASSIGNMENT 18

Step 5: Composing—Choose your audience (Who will read your review?) and then begin to draft your piece. Try to ignore the critic in your mind and just get down the words. I call this the "down draft." Remember that we rarely publish our first draft. Take a break and give the draft a rest. Then, begin the second draft. I call this the "up draft" because you are going to fix it up. If you can't find anything to fix, ask someone else to read the draft. When the second draft is finished, it is time to work on the third draft. This is the "heavy" draft where you make sure you have plenty of content. Content is essential to a good book review. Share some important information, add some quotations, or relate the book to another you have read.

Step 6: Revision—Revise, revise, revise. Edit your piece carefully before submission. Ask someone to read the piece—once for understanding and once for grammatical errors and spelling. Practice using the rubric. Make the necessary changes and send the review with a short cover letter to your selected journal editor.

What Does a "Ready to Submit" Book Review Look Like?

Before beginning your practice exercise in book-review writing, take a look at the following example of a review, which follows the guidelines from *The Reading Teacher*. It was written by Barbara S. Vought, Cape Fear Community College, Wilmington, North Carolina, USA. It seems obvious to me that this reviewer has had many "conversations" with this author.

> Barbara Elleman. 1999. *Tomie dePaola: His art and his stories*. G.P. Putnam's Sons (345 Hudson Street, New York, NY 10014, USA). 218 pp. ISBN 0-399-23129. Hardcover. US$35.00.
>
> Everyone loves the illustrations of Tomie dePaola. To have a biography filled with his art is truly a joy. Learning the role of family, friends, and experiences in his career is interesting, learning the part played by gardening and cooking is fascinating, learning his methods, growth, and accomplishments is engrossing. Reading this book, however, takes a back seat to looking at the pictures; one becomes a child again and looks through that child's eyes to the end of the book. And, then, we want more!
>
>   Scenes from Tomie dePaola's childhood abound in his illustrations and in his stories. His grandmothers even look much like the characters in Nana Upstairs & Nana Downstairs, a story woven from his past. His grandfather, his parents, his sister, all find places in his art, simply, it seems, because they have places in his heart. His personal experiences figure strongly in The Art Lesson and Oliver Button Is a Sissy. We are thankful dePaola persevered in spite of peer pressure.
>
>   Pictures of Tomie dePaola's home and garden, featuring the illustrator/author with his family, friends, and pets, show the reader how closely his life connects to his books. His colors

seem to come directly from his gardens; the faces of his dogs grace more than a few children's books; and a white bow in his mother's hair and her dress are there on young Marianna May in the book Marianna May and Nursey.

Barbara Elleman's clever techniques of quoting dePaola adds interest as well as understanding. For example, young Strega Nona's Grandma, Concetta tells her, "You must blow three kisses and the pot will stop. For that is the ingrediente segreto—LOVE. It is the same with all your magic. Always Love." This she points out is dePaola's basic contention because "Children," dePaola says, "are the hope of our future, and we must treat them as such. This may sound trite, but it's true." Inserted in the middle of the book is an essay written by dePaola, "Tomie, Where Do You Get Your Ideas?" Another strategy Elleman uses is to point out dePaola's art techniques, which a nonartist may miss, as she tells the stories that match the illustrations that the reader "reads" a second time.

An art gallery of non-book works and an essay from one of dePaola's college professors end the book, telling us more about the man and his work than any biography could have told without it. The reader finishes by looking at the pictures once again, and she realizes that she loves the man as well as his illustrations—the two cannot be separated. *Tomie dePaola: His Art and His Stories* is a beautiful book for the child in all of us.

Now, just for fun, let's look at a different kind of book review in Figure 8. This review was created by Debora Misencik, one of my graduate students several years ago. You may think that Debora got stuck on the graphic representation part of Step 3 in Assignment 17 (page 69), but her review gives the reader lots of information. It is creative and innovative, and the reviewer was very efficient with PowerPoint. We certainly can grasp an overview of the content and organization quickly with a visual summary.

FIGURE 8
BOOK REVIEW IN VISUAL SUMMARY BY DEBORA MISENCIK

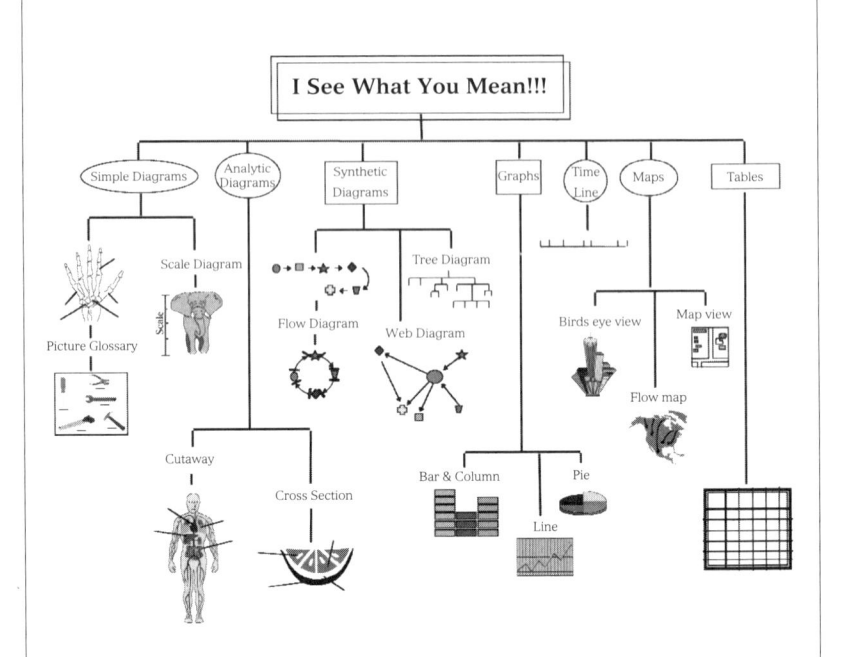

Steve Moline. 1995. *I see what you mean*. Stenhouse Publishers (226 York Street, York, Maine 03909, USA). 148 pp. ISBN 1-57110-031-8. Softcover. US$21.50.

How Can I Assess My Own Review?

I use a rubric for a quick, holistic assessment (see Figure 9). This is the same rubric I use with students and with others who submit book reviews to me for publication. Try it out on your book review.

FIGURE 9
BOOK REVIEW RUBRIC

3 Excellent Review
- Targeted to specific audience and journal
- Well organized, clear, and grammatically correct
- Synthesized information with vitality and grace
- Covered content comprehensively and accurately

2 Effective Review
- Limited audience, but no specific journal
- Well organized with few errors in mechanics and grammar
- Summarized information creatively and concisely
- Covered content accurately

1 Developing Review
- No specified audience or journal
- Organized with many errors in mechanics and grammar
- Reported information with little attention to detail
- Covered content superficially

What Did I Learn?

Moving from private to public writing involves taking a risk. However, if you agree that writing for publication might make you a better teacher and thinker, it is time to get started on your first publication. Practice the publication process by preparing and submitting a book review for publication. You understand why a book review is a logical place to start. You know your target audience. You have reviewed the process, you know how to self-assess a book review, and you have seen examples of the end product. The time has come to follow the recommended approach or develop your own approach and write your first publication. I just know it will be a great success!

APPENDIX

Sample Charts, Guidelines, and Letters

DIFFERENT KINDS OF THINKING CHART   80

THINKING WORDS CHART   81

HIGHER ORDER THINKING CHART   82

SIX STEPS TO WRITING A SUCCESSFUL BOOK REVIEW   83

SAMPLE COVER LETTER   84

SAMPLE QUERY LETTER   85

DIFFERENT KINDS OF THINKING

Find examples in your writing, highlight with an orange marker, and record them below.

Basic Thinking
-
-
-

Critical Thinking
-
-
-

Creative Thinking
-
-
-

Reflective Thinking
-
-
-

Parallel Thinking
-
-
-

Fuzzy Thinking
-
-
-

THINKING WORDS

Find examples in your writing, highlight with a green marker, and record them below.

Easy Words	Difficult Words	Challenging Words

HIGHER ORDER THINKING

Find examples in your writing, highlight with a yellow marker, and record them below.

Knowledge: Recalling and remembering information
-
-
-
-

Comprehension: Understanding information
-
-
-
-

Application: Adapting or using information
-
-
-
-

Analysis: Dividing information into parts
-
-
-
-

Synthesis: Integrating and creating new information
-
-
-
-

Evaluation: Judging the value of information
-
-
-
-

SIX STEPS TO WRITING A SUCCESSFUL BOOK REVIEW

Step 1: **Annotation**
Highlight or underline as you read the text. Make comments or ask questions in the book margins.

Step 2: **Note taking**
Record important and/or interesting quotations and ideas in your notebook or journal. Stay close to the text. Indicate exact page numbers in your notebook. Add your own thoughts as your mind makes automatic connections for you.

Step 3: **Illustrating**
Draw a graphic or visual representation of the whole book. Take a look from the balcony to see the "big picture." (Close your eyes and pretend you are looking at the situation from a higher place.) A different perspective can give you insight.

Step 4: **Making meaning**
Think about the practical applications and usefulness of the content in the text as you extend your interpretation. Try reading some of your favorite parts aloud. Spend some time thinking and allow your brain to "bubble." This may help you find direction for your writing.

Step 5: **Composing**
Choose your audience (Who will read your review?) and then begin to draft your piece. Try to ignore the critic in your mind and just get down the words. I call this the "down draft." Remember that we rarely publish our first draft. Take a break and give the draft a rest. Then, begin the second draft. I call this the "up draft" because you are going to fix it up. If you can't find anything to fix, ask someone else to read the draft. When the second draft is finished, it is time to work on the third draft. This is the "heavy" draft where you make sure you have plenty of content. Content is essential to a good book review. Share some important information, add some quotations, or relate the book to another you have read.

Step 6: **Revision**
Revise, revise, revise. Edit your piece carefully before submission. Ask someone to read the piece—once for understanding and once for grammatical errors and spelling. Make the necessary changes and send the review with a short cover letter to a selected journal editor.

SAMPLE COVER LETTER

Street Address
City, State Zip
Date

Editor's Name, Editor
Journal's Name (underline or italicize)
Street Address
City, State Zip

Dear (Editor's Name):

As a middle school English teacher for the past 12 years, I have read many books on portfolio assessment. I have just finished reading _____ (insert the publication date in parentheses), written by _____, and I have prepared a 400-word review of this book.

I hope you will consider publishing my review in your upcoming themed issue on portfolios. I look forward to hearing whether you are interested in my manuscript. Thank you for your consideration.

Sincerely,

Your Name
E-mail Address (optional)

Enclosure

SAMPLE QUERY LETTER

Street Address
City, State Zip
Date

Editor's Name, Editor
Journal's Name (underline or all caps)
Street Address
City, State Zip

Dear (Editor's Name):

As a middle school English teacher for the past 12 years, I have read many books on portfolio assessment. I have just finished reading _____ (insert the publication date in parentheses), written by _____, and I wonder if your journal would be interested in publishing a 400-word review of this current publication on portfolios.

I look forward to hearing whether you are interested in such a manuscript. Thank you for your consideration.

Sincerely,

Your Name
E-mail Address (optional)

REFERENCES

Aslett, D., & Cartaino, C. (2001). *Get organized, get published: 225 ways to make time for success.* Cincinnati, OH: Writer's Digest Books.

Baumann, J., & Johnson, D. (1991). *Writing for publication in reading and language arts.* Newark, DE: International Reading Association.

Bender, S. (Ed.). (1997). *The writer's journal: 40 contemporary writers and their journals.* New York: Bantam Doubleday Dell.

Berger, A. (1997). Writing about reading for the public. *The Reading Teacher, 51,* 6–10.

Beyer, B. (1997). *Improving student thinking: A comprehensive approach.* Boston: Allyn & Bacon.

Bloom, B. (1956). *Taxonomy of educational objectives: The classification of educational goals* (Handbook 1: Cognitive domain). New York: Longmans, Green.

Booth, W.C., Colomb, G.C., & Williams, J. (1995). *The craft of research.* Chicago: The University of Chicago Press.

Burack, S.K. (Ed.). (2001). *The writer's handbook 2001.* Boston: The Writer.

Burnaford, G.E., Fischer, J.C., & Hobson, D. (Eds.). (2001). *Teachers doing research: The power of action through inquiry* (2nd ed.). Mahwah, NJ: Erlbaum.

Cabell, D., & English, D. (1998). *Cabell's directory of publishing opportunities in education* (5th ed.). Beaumont, TX: Cabell.

Calkins, L.M. (1994). *The art of teaching writing.* Portsmouth, NH: Heinemann.

Campbell, D.M., Cignetti, P.B., Melenyzer, B.J., Nettles, D., & Wyman, R. (1997). *How to develop a professional portfolio: A manual for teachers.* Boston: Allyn & Bacon.

Chaffee, J. (1998). *The thinker's way: 8 steps to a richer life.* New York: Little, Brown.

Cheney, T.A.R. (1987). *Writing creative nonfiction: How to use fiction techniques to make your nonfiction more interesting, dramatic, and vivid.* Cincinnati, OH: Writer's Digest Books.

Christenbury, L. (2000). *Making the journey: Being and becoming a teacher of English language arts* (2nd ed.). Portsmouth, NH: Heinemann.

Clark, T., Woods, B., Blocksom, P., & Terez, A. (Eds.). (1997). *The Writer's Digest guide to good writing*. Cincinnati, OH. Writer's Digest Books.

Courtney, A.M., & Abodeeb, T.L. (2001). *Journey of discovery: Building a classroom community through diagnostic-reflective portfolios*. Newark, DE: International Reading Association.

Covey, S.R. (1989). *The 7 habits of highly effective people: Powerful lessons in personal change*. New York: Simon & Schuster.

Cramer, R.L. (2001). *Creative power: The nature and nurture of children's writing*. New York: Longman.

Crowe, C. (1992). Why write for publication? In K.L. Dahl (Ed.), *Teacher as writer: Entering the professional conversation* (pp. 74–80). Urbana, IL: National Council of Teachers of English.

Dahl, K.L. (Ed.). (1992). *Teacher as writer: Entering the professional conversation*. Urbana, IL: National Council of Teachers of English.

Daniels, H., Bizar, M., & Zemelman, S. (2001). *Rethinking high school: Best practice in teaching, learning, and leadership*. Portsmouth, NH: Heinemann.

De Bono, E. (1999). *Six thinking hats*. Boston: Little, Brown.

Dewey, J. (1997). *How we think: A restatement of the relation of reflective thinking to the educative process*. Boston: Henry Holt.

Dillard, A. (1989). *The writing life*. New York: HarperCollins.

Edelstein, S. (1993). *30 steps to becoming a writer and getting published: The complete starter kit for aspiring writers*. Cincinnati, OH. Writer's Digest Books.

Elbow, P. (1986). *Writing without teachers* (2nd ed.). London: Oxford University Press.

Emerson, C. (1993). *The 30-minute writer: How to write and sell short pieces*. Cincinnati, OH: Writer's Digest Books.

Erwin, R., Jr. (1992). Reviewing books for scholarly journals. In J.M. Moxley (Ed.), *Writing and publishing for academic authors* (pp. 111–118). New York: University Press of America.

Fulwiler, T. (1987). *Teaching with writing*. Portsmouth, NH: Boynton/Cook.

Germano, W. (2001). *Getting it published: A guide for scholars and anyone else serious about serious books*. Chicago: The University of Chicago Press.

Glasser, W. (1985). *Positive addiction*. New York: Harper & Row.

Glatthorn, A. (1996). *The teacher's portfolio: Fostering and documenting professional development*. Rockport, MA: ProActive Publications.

Grace, M. (1999). Be a better writer, be a better teacher. *Journal of Adolescent & Adult Literacy, 43,* 60–62.

Gregorian, V. (2001). Teacher education must become colleges' central preoccupation. *The Chronicle of Higher Education, 47*(49), B7–B8.

Heard, G. (1995). *Writing toward home: Tales and lessons to find your way.* Portsmouth, NH: Heinemann.

Henson, K.T. (1991). *Writing for successful publication.* Bloomington, IN: ERIC Clearinghouse on Reading and Communication Skills.

Henson, K.T. (1995). *The art of writing for publication.* Boston: Allyn & Bacon.

Henson, K.T. (1999). *Writing for professional publication: Keys to academic and business success.* Boston: Allyn & Bacon.

Hillocks, G., Jr. (1995). *Teaching writing as reflective practice.* New York: Teachers College Press.

Hobson, D. (2001). Action and reflection: Narrative and journaling in teacher research. In G.E. Burnaford, J.C. Fischer, & D. Hobson (Eds.), *Teachers doing research: The power of action through inquiry* (2nd ed., pp. 7–27). Mahwah, NJ: Erlbaum.

Holmes, M. (1993). *Writing articles from the heart: How to write and sell your life experiences.* Cincinnati, OH: Writer's Digest Books.

Judy, S. (1982). *Publishing in English education.* Portsmouth, NH: Boynton/Cook.

Katz, S.B., Kapes, J.T., & Zirkel, P.A. (1980). *Resources for writing for publication in education.* New York: Teachers College Press.

Klauser, H.A. (2000). *Write it down, make it happen: Knowing what you want—and getting it.* New York: Scribner.

Lamott, A. (1994). *Bird by bird: Some instructions on writing and life.* New York: Random House.

Larsen, M. (1997). *How to write a book proposal* (2nd ed.). Cincinnati, OH: Writer's Digest Books.

Levy, M. (2000). *Accidental genius: Revolutionize your thinking through private writing.* San Francisco, CA: Berrett-Koehler.

McLaughlin, M., Vogt, M.E., Anderson, J.A., DuMez, J., Peter, M.G., & Hunter, A. (1998). *Professional portfolio models: Reflections across the teaching profession.* Norwood, MA: Christopher-Gordon.

Merkley, D.M., & Jefferies, D. (2000/2001). Guidelines for implementing a graphic organizer. *The Reading Teacher, 54,* 350–357.

Morgenstern, J. (1998). *Organizing from the inside out: The foolproof system for organizing your home, your office, and your life.* New York: Henry Holt.

Murray, D.M. (1984). *Write to learn.* New York: Holt, Rinehart and Winston.

Murray, D.M. (1985). The essential delay: When writer's block isn't. In M. Rose (Ed.), *When writers can't write* (pp. 219–226). London: Guilford.

Murray, D.M. (1996). *Crafting a life in essay, story, poem.* Portsmouth, NH: Heinemann.

Murray, D.M. (2000). *Writing to deadline: The journalist at work.* Portsmouth, NH: Heinemann.

Nuwer, H. (1995). *How to write like an expert about anything.* Cincinnati, OH: Writer's Digest Books.

Olson, G. (1992). Publishing scholarship in humanistic disciplines: Joining the conversation. In J.M. Moxley (Ed.), *Writing and publishing for academic authors* (pp. 49–69). New York: University Press of America.

Patterson, L., Santa, C.M., Short, K.G., & Smith, K. (Eds.). (1993). *Teachers are researchers: Reflection and action.* Newark, DE: International Reading Association.

Perkins, D.N. (1995). *Outsmarting your IQ: The emerging science of learnable intelligences.* New York: The Free Press.

Polking, K. (1987). *A beginner's guide to getting published.* Cincinnati, OH: Writer's Digest Books.

Poynter, D. (2000). *Successful nonfiction: Tips & inspiration for getting published.* Santa Barbara, CA: Para Publishing.

Reid, L., & Golub, J. (Eds.). (1999). *Reflective activities: Helping students connect with texts.* Urbana, IL: National Council of Teachers of English.

Reno, D.E. (2000). *The unofficial guide to managing time.* Chicago: IDG.

Rogers, S.E., & Danielson, K.E. (1996). *Teacher portfolios: Literary artifacts and themes.* Portsmouth, NH: Heinemann.

Schon, D.A. (1983). *The reflective practitioner.* New York: Basic Books.

Sebranek, P., Kemper, D., & Meyer, V. (2001). *Writers Inc.: A student handbook for writing & learning.* Wilmington, MA: Write Source.

Sebranek, P., Meyer, V., & Kemper, D. (1997). *Write for college: A student handbook.* Wilmington, MA: Write Source.

Seifert, K.L. (1999). *Reflective thinking and professional development.* Boston: Houghton Mifflin.

Sizer, T.R. (1997). *Horace's hope: What works for the American high school*. Boston: Houghton Mifflin.

Slifkin, J.M. (2001). Writing the care of the self: Higher order thinking in reflective journals. *English Leadership Quarterly, 24*, 5–9.

Stangl, J. (1994). *How to get your teaching ideas published: A writer's guide to educational publishing*. New York: Walker.

Tafel, L.S., & Fischer, J.C. (2001). Teacher action research and professional development: Foundations for educational renewal. In G.E. Burnaford, J.C. Fischer, & D. Hobson (Eds.), *Teachers doing research: The power of action through inquiry* (2nd ed., pp. 221–235). Mahwah, NJ: Erlbaum.

Tishman, S., & Perkins, D.N. (1997). The language of thinking. *Phi Delta Kappan, 78*, 368–371.

White, E. (1985). *Teaching and assessing writing*. San Francisco, CA: Jossey-Bass.

Wiggins, G., & McTighe, J. (1998). *Understanding by design*. Alexandria, VA: Association for Supervision and Curriculum Development.

Wilcox, B.L. (1996). Getting published: Private to public writing. *The Reading Teacher, 49*, 360–365.

Wilcox, B.L. (1997). The teacher's portfolio: An essential tool for professional development. *The Reading Teacher, 51*, 170–173.

Wilcox, B.L. (1998). Thinking journals. *The Reading Teacher, 51*, 350–353.

Wilcox, B.L., & Tomei, L. (1999a). Assessing teacher performance with a portfolio rubric. *English Leadership Quarterly, 22*(2), 6–10.

Wilcox, B.L., & Tomei, L. (1999b). *Professional portfolios for teachers: A guide for learners, experts, and scholars*. Norwood, MA: Christopher-Gordon.

Wilcox, B.L., & Wojnar, L.C. (2000, August). Best practice goes online. *Reading Online*. Available: http://www.readingonline.org/articles/art_index.asp?HREF=/articles/wilcox/index.html

Wojnar, L.C. (2000). *Instructional design and implementation of a best practice model of online teaching and learning*. Unpublished dissertation, Duquesne University, Pittsburgh, PA.

INDEX

Note: Page references followed by *f* indicate figures.

A
ABODEEB, T.L., 27, 88
ACTION, 27
ACTION RESEARCH, 15
ADVICE, 55–58
ANALYSIS, 35–36, 36f
ANDERSON, J.A., 23, 89
ANNOTATION, 67, 68, 68f, 83
APPLICATION, 35–36, 36f
ASLETT, D., 5, 12, 87
ASSESSMENT: self-assessment scale, 45–46; of your own review, 76–77
ASSISTANT PROFESSORS, 4
ASSOCIATION FOR SUPERVISION AND CURRICULUM DEVELOPMENT, 62
ATTITUDE, 39; toward learning, 46
AUDIENCE, 70–73
AUTHORITIES, 45
AUTHORS, 28

B
BAUMANN, J., 8, 87
BEGINNING WRITING, 10–12
BENDER, S., 20, 87
BERGER, ALLEN, 9, 87
"BEST PRACTICE" LESSONS, 15
BEYER, B., 35, 40, 42, 87
BIZAR, M., 40, 88
BLOCKSOM, P., 55, 88
BLOOM, B., 35, 87
BLOOM'S TAXONOMY, 35–36, 36f
BOOK EDITORS, 5
BOOK PROPOSALS, 59
BOOK PUBLISHERS, 63
BOOK PUBLISHING GUIDELINES, 63
BOOK REVIEWS, 65; assessing, 76–77; composing, 70–73; developing, 77f; effective, 77f; essential ingredients of, 71; excellent, 77f; example, 74–75, 76f; versus generic writing, 68–69, 68f; introduction, 72; publishing, 68–69; rationale for writing, 66–67; "ready to submit," 74–76; rubric for, 77f; sample, 71–72; steps in writing, 67, 69, 73, 83; target audience for, 70–71; why begin with, 66–67; writing, 65–77
BOOKS: literacy learning, 55; Writer's Digest books, 55
BOOTH, W.C., 59, 87
BURACK, S.K., 63, 87
BURNAFORD, G.E., 59, 87

C

CABELL, D., 63, 87
CABELL'S DIRECTORY OF PUBLISHING OPPORTUNITIES IN EDUCATION (CABELL & ENGLISH), 63
CALKINS, L.M., 9, 87
CAMPBELL, D.M., 71, 87
CARTAINO, C., 5, 12, 87
CHAFFEE, J., 42, 44, 45, 87
CHARTS: Different Kinds of Thinking, 80; Higher Order Thinking, 82; Thinking Words, 81
CHENEY, T.A.R., 55, 87
CHRISTENBURY, L., viii, 87
CIGNETTI, P.B., 71, 87
CLARITY OF WRITING, 54
CLARK, T., 55, 88
COGNITION, 35–36, 36f; higher order thinking, 35–37; Higher Order Thinking chart, 82
COLOMB, G.C., 59, 87
COMMITMENT, 27
COMPOSING, 68f, 69, 70–73, 83
COMPREHENSION, 35–36, 36f
CONCLUSIONS, 33
CONSTRUCTING MEANING, 28–29
CONSTRUCTIVE CRITICISM, 57
CONVERSATIONS: with authors, 28; with others, 28; professional, 59; to record in thinking journals, 28; with self, 28
COURTNEY, A.M., 27, 88
COVER LETTER, 73, 84
COVEY, S.R., 10, 12–13, 26, 27, 88
CRAMER, R.L., 4, 5, 88
CREATIVE THINKING, 31, 32f
CRITICAL THINKING, 31, 32f, 45
CROWE, C., 9, 88
CURRENT PROJECT (FOLDER), 50

D

DAHL, K.L., 8, 88
DAILY WRITING, 18–19
DANIELS, H., 40, 88
DANIELSON, K.E., 23, 72, 90
DE BONO, E., 32f, 88
DEMONSTRATING, 15, 29, 30
DEPAOLA, TOMIE, 73–74
DESIRE (WANT TO DO), 12–13
DEVELOPING WRITING PROJECTS, 52–54
DEWEY, JOHN, 27, 39, 88
DIFFERENT KINDS OF THINKING CHART, 80
DILLARD, A., 22, 56, 88
DRAFTING, 71–73
DUMEZ, J., 23, 89

E

"EATING AN ELEPHANT," 68–69
EDELSTEIN, S., 55, 88
EDUCATIONAL LEADERSHIP, 62
EDUCATIONAL RESOURCES INFORMATION CENTER (ERIC), 61–62
EDUCATION JOURNALS, 56
EDUCATION ORGANIZATIONS, 59
ELBOW, PETER, 3, 24, 55, 88
ELECTRONIC DISKS, 50
ELECTRONIC JOURNALS, 62
ELECTRONIC MAILING LISTS, 56
ELLEMAN, BARBARA, 74–75
EMERSON, C., 55, 69, 88
ENGLISH, D., 63, 87
ENGLISH JOURNAL, 62
ERIC (EDUCATIONAL RESOURCES INFORMATION CENTER), 61–62
ERWIN, R., JR., 65, 88
EVALUATION: assessing your own review, 77; of evidence, 45; level of Bloom's taxonomy, 35–36, 36f; self-assessment scale, 45–46
EVIDENCE: evaluation of, 45; factual, 45; of thinking, 30–37
EXCUSES FOR NOT WRITING, 5–7
EXHIBITION, 15; evidence of, 30; power of, 40. *See also* Demonstration
EXPERIENCE, 45
EXPERTISE, 13–17

F

FACTUAL EVIDENCE, 45
FALLACIES OF THINKING, 44
FAULTY THINKING, 44
FISCHER, J.C., 56, 59, 87, 91
FOLDERS, 50
FULWILER, TOBY, 3, 55, 88
FUZZY THINKING, 25, 31, 32f, 44

G

GERMANO, W., 6–7, 88
GLASSER, W., 10, 88
GLATTHORN, A., 71–72, 88
GOALS, 18–19; setting, 12, 51
GOLUB, J., 23, 90
GRACE, M., 1, 9, 89
GRAVES, DONALD, 29
GREGORIAN, V., 2, 89
GUIDELINES, 63

H

HABIT(S): changing, 5, 17–20; of mind, 37–41; nurturing, 37–41; suggestions for developing or improving, 10; writing, 1, 22
HEARD, G., 54, 89
HEMINGWAY, ERNEST, 22
HENSON, K.T., 1, 8, 89
HIGHER ORDER THINKING, 35–37; Higher Order Thinking chart, 82
HILLOCKS, G., JR., 15–16, 89
HOBSON, D., 37, 38, 59, 87, 89
HOLMES, M., 4, 19, 55, 89
HUNTER, A., 23, 89

I

ILLUSTRATING, 68, 68f, 69, 83
INTEGRATING LITERACIES, 14, 28–30
INTERACTING, 15, 29, 30
INTERNATIONAL EDUCATION ORGANIZATIONS, 63
INTERNATIONAL READING ASSOCIATION (IRA), 61–62
INTERNET, 31; electronic journals, 62; electronic mailing lists, 56; research on, 53; websites of education organizations, 63
INVESTIGATIONS, 33

J

JEFFERIES, D., 40, 89
JOHNSON, D., 8, 87
JOURNAL OF ADOLESCENT & ADULT LITERACY, 62
JOURNAL PUBLISHERS, 62–63
JOURNALS, PERSONAL, 18–19; strength of, 37; writing in, 23–24, 25. *See also* Journals, thinking
JOURNALS, PROFESSIONAL: education, 56, 62; electronic, 62; refereed, 56
JOURNALS, THINKING, 22, 26–30; conversations to record in, 28; My Thinking Journal (folder), 50
JUDY, S., 8, 89
JUNIOR PROFESSORS, 4

K

KAPES, J.T., 8, 89
KATZ, S.B., 8, 89
KEMPER, D., 44, 66, 90
KINDERGARTEN MODEL OF ORGANIZATION, 64
KLAUSER, H.A., 51, 89
KNOWLEDGE: building a knowledge base, 28, 29; level of Bloom's taxonomy, 35–36, 36f; monitoring ways of knowing, 41–46; what to do and why, 10–11

L

LAMOTT, A., 39, 47, 89
LARSEN, M., 55, 89

LEARNING, 27; attitude toward, 46; "best practice" lessons, 15; reading to learn, 38; representing to learn, 51
LEARNING HOW TO WRITE, vii, viii
LEVY, M., 25, 89
LINDEMANN, ERIKA, 3
LITERACY INTEGRATION, 14, 28–30

M

MAUGHAM, SOMERSET, 17
MCLAUGHLIN, M., 23, 71–72, 89
MCTIGHE, J., 39, 91
MEANING MAKING, 28–29, 68, 68f, 69, 83
MELENYZER, B.J., 71, 87
MENTORS, 56
MERKLEY, D.M., 40, 89
MEYER, V., 44, 66, 90
MISENCIK, DEBORA, 75, 76f
MOLINE, S., 76f
MONITORING WAYS OF KNOWING, 41–46
MORGENSTERN, J., 64, 90
MURRAY, DONALD M., vii, viii, 1, 3, 6, 7, 12, 21, 22, 38, 55, 90
MY PUBLISHED PIECES (FOLDER), 50
MY THINKING JOURNAL (FOLDER), 50

N–O

NATIONAL COUNCIL OF TEACHERS OF ENGLISH (NCTE), 62, 63
NATIONAL EDUCATION ORGANIZATIONS, 62–63
NATIONAL WRITING PROJECT, 3, 56
NEGATIVE TRANSFER, 44
NETTLES, D., 71, 87
NOTE TAKING, 68, 68f, 69, 83
NURTURING HABITS OF MIND, 37–41
NUWER, H., 55, 90
OLSON, G., 4, 90
ORGANIZATION, 19; Kindergarten Model of Organization, 64; of writing, 49–64

P–Q

PARALLEL THINKING, 31. 32f
PATTERSON, L., 8, 90
PERFECTIONISM, 39
PERKINS, D.N., 23, 33, 44, 90, 91
PERSONAL EXPERIENCE, 45
PETER, M.G., 23, 89
POLKING, K., 55, 90
PORTFOLIO POSTERS, 51, 52f
PORTFOLIOS, 50–52; sharing, 51
POSITIVE ADDICTION (GLASSER), 10, 89

POSTERS, 51, 52*f*
POWERPOINT (SOFTWARE), 76
POYNTER, D., 67, 90
PREPARATION FOR PUBLICATION, 53–54
PREWRITING, 21, 71
PROFESSIONAL CONVERSATIONS, 60
PROFESSIONAL DEVELOPMENT, 64
PUBLICATION: author's journey to, 2–5; benefits of, 20; of book reviews, 68–69; first published writing, 4; guidelines on book publishing, 63; kinds of published writing, 58–60; My Published Pieces (folder), 50; outlets for, 60–63; preparation for, 53–54; readiness for, 17–19; reasons for, 1; submission for, 50, 74–76, 83; by teachers, 5–6; unwritten rule of, 54
PUBLICATIONS, 62–63
PUBLISHERS, 60–63
QUALITY OF WRITING, 54
QUERY LETTER, 73, 85

R
READINESS: for submission, 74–76; for writing, 17–19
READING, 14, 29, 30; to learn, 38; vocabulary for, 34*f*, 34–35
READING ONLINE, 62
READING RESOURCES (FOLDER), 50
THE READING TEACHER, 61, 62
REFEREED JOURNALS, 56
REFERENCES, 45
REFLECTION, 14, 22, 27, 31, 32*f*; as journal entry, 23–24; recommended strategy for, 23; on reflections, 37
REHEARSING, 21
REID, L., 23, 90
RENEWAL, 29
RENO, D.E., 6, 17, 90
REPRESENTING TO LEARN, 51
RESEARCH, 59; action, 15; on Internet, 53; writing, 59, 60
RESOURCES, 8–9; Reading Resources (folder), 50; Writer's Digest books, 55
REVIEWERS, 56
REVIEWS. *See* Book reviews
REVISION, 68*f*, 69, 73, 83
RICO, GABRIELE, 3
RIEF, LINDA, 3
RISK TAKING, 39
ROGERS, S.E., 23, 72, 90
RULES OF PUBLICATION, 54

S
SAMPLE COVER LETTER, 84
SAMPLE QUERY LETTER, 85
SANTA, C.M., 8, 90
SCHOLARSHIP, 29

Schon, D.A., 27, 90
Sebranek, P., 44, 66, 90
Seifert, K.L., 23, 49, 90
self-assessment scale, 45–46
self-conversations, 28
sharing portfolios, 51
sharing writing, 49–64
Short, K.G., 8, 90
Silverstein, Shel, 68
Sizer, T.R., 40, 91
skill (how to do), 11
Slifkin, J.M., 35, 91
Smith, K., 8, 90
speaking vocabulary, 34f, 34–35
spiral, upward, 27
Stangl, J., 8, 91
submission for publication, 68f, 69, 73, 83; "ready to submit" book reviews, 74–76; Submitted Pieces (folder), 50
support, 55–58
support groups, 56
suspicion, 33
synthesis, 35–36, 36f

T–U
Tafel, L.S., 56, 91
target audience, 70–71
taxonomy, 35–36, 36f
teachers: as researchers, 60; writing for publication by, 5–6
Teachers Doing Research: The Power of Action Through Inquiry (Burnaford, Fischer, & Hobson), 60
Terez, A., 55, 88
thinking, 14, 29, 30; basic, 31, 32f; creative, 31, 32f; critical, 31, 32f, 45; different kinds of, 31–33, 32f, 80; evidence of, 30–37; fallacies of, 44; faulty, 44; fuzzy, 25, 31, 32f, 44; higher order, 35–37, 82; parallel, 31, 32f; quality of, 41; reflective, 27, 31, 32f; rubric for, 42–44, 43f; about thinking, 23, 46; visible, 22–26, 28; and writing, 21–47
thinking journals, 22, 26–30; conversations to record in, 28; My Thinking Journal (folder), 50. *See also* Journals, personal
thinking vocabulary, 33–35; Thinking Words chart, 81; word list, 34f
Tishman, S., 33, 91
Tomei, L., 27, 51, 91
unwritten rule of publication, 54
upward spiral, 27

V
viewing, 15, 29, 30; evidence of, 30; power of exhibition, 40. *See also* Demonstration
visible thinking, 22–26, 28
vision, 22

VOCABULARY: reading, 34f, 34–35; speaking, 34f, 34–35; thinking, 33–35, 34f; Thinking Words chart, 81; writing, 34f, 34–35
VOGT, M.E., 23, 71–72, 89
VOUGHT, BARBARA S., 74–75
VYGOTSKY, LEV, 40

W–Z
WHITE, E., 45, 91
WIGGINS, G., 39, 91
WILCOX, B.L., 4, 14, 20, 27, 51, 70, 71, 91
WILLIAMS, J., 59, 87
WOJNAR, L.C., 14, 35, 91
WOODS, B., 55, 88
WORKSHOPS, 56
WRITERS: becoming a writer, 1–20; being and becoming, viii; novice, 55; Writer's Digest books valuable for, 55
WRITER'S BLOCK, 67
WRITER'S DIGEST BOOKS, 55
THE WRITER'S HANDBOOK (BURACK), 63
WRITING, 15–17, 29, 30; advice for, 55–58; benefits of, 20; book review, 65–77; clarity of, 54; daily, 1, 18–19; desire for (want to do), 12–13; evidence of, 30; excuses for not writing, 5–7; generic, 68–69, 68f; goals for, 18–19; as habit, 1; journal, 23, 25; knowledge of (what to do and why), 10–11; learning how to write, vii, viii; order of, 66; organizing, 49–64; preparation for publication, 53–54; private, 11, 38; process of, 22, 66; publication of, 2–5; published, 58–60; quality of, 54; readiness for, 17–19; reading to learn from, 38; reasons for, 1; reflective, 23; rehearsing, 21; research, 59; sharing, ix, 49–64; skill (how to do), 11; support for, 55–58; by teachers, 5–6; thinking and, viii, 21–47; as vision, 22; where to begin, 10–12
WRITING BUDDY, 7, 56
WRITING CLASSES, 56
WRITING GROUPS, 56
WRITING HABIT(S), 22; suggestions for developing or improving, 10; where to begin, 10–12
WRITING IDEAS (FOLDER), 50
WRITING PORTFOLIO, 50–52; artifacts in, 50; sharing, 51
WRITING PORTFOLIO POSTER, 51, 52f
WRITING PROJECTS: Current Project (folder), 50; developing, 52–54; questions to ask as you begin, 53
WRITING VOCABULARY, 34f, 34–35
WRITTEN REFERENCES, 45
WYMAN, R., 71, 87
ZEMELMAN, S., 40, 88
ZIRKEL, P.A., 8, 89